# I REFUSE
## MEMORIES OF A VIETNAM WAR OBJECTOR

## DONALD L. SIMONS

**THE BROKEN RIFLE PRESS, Trenton, New Jersey**

**I REFUSE**
**memories of a Vietnam war objector**

Requests to republish parts of *I Refuse* should be addressed to:
BROKEN RIFLE PRESS, PO Box 749, Trenton, NJ 08607, USA.

Simons, Donald L.
I Refuse.

1. Vietnamese conflict, 1961–1975—personal narrative, American.
2. Conscientious objection. Pacifism. Antiwar movement.

Includes bibliographical references and resource list.


The Preface quote appears in *Conscripts of Conscience,* © 1972
R. Alfred Hassler. Reprinted through the courtesy of Garland
Publishing Company, New York, New York.

Printed in the United States of America.
This publication is printed on acid-free paper.

Cover by: Harold Shull Associates. East Brunswick, NJ.

Photograph by: Brad Kellar. La Habra, CA.

Library of Congress Catalog Card Number: 91–070992.

ISBN: 0-9620024-2-9 Hardcover.
ISBN: 0-9620024-3-7 Softcover.

# CONTENTS

# PREFACE

Grapes cannot be gathered from thorns.
Nor can figs from thistles.
Good ends are *not* achieved by evil means.
It is *not* possible to create a world of brotherhood
by hating and slaughtering our brothers.

—R. Alfred Hassler

# INTRODUCTION

This book tells one man's story. In certain ways, every person who confronted the draft during the Vietnam War, or at any other time, has a unique tale to tell. Such an individual faces questions that ultimately are answered in the lonely passages of the human conscience, and no two people find their ways through those passages by precisely the same path.

In another sense, though, Donald Simons' story is part of the story of hundreds of thousands of conscientious objectors, draft resisters, and peace activists. He was part of a mass movement for social change, a movement that embodies a tradition and a history. Considered from this perspective, one person's refusal to fight is part of an enormous mosaic that stretches not only across this vast nation, but also back in time. Most Americans associate the terms "conscientious objector" (CO) and "draft resister"* with the Vietnam War. The real story of such individuals, however, is far broader than that. Men have "conscientiously objected" to military service in what is now the United States for far longer than the United States has been a nation.

What follows is not intended to explain the anguish, the uncertainty, the courage or the suffering of the men and women who say "I refuse" to war. Rather, this introduction seeks to

---

*"Conscientious objector" describes any person whom the government exempts from armed military service because he or she is opposed to "participation in war in any form" due to deeply held religious or moral beliefs. Such persons have often been required to perform civilian service. There is no single definition of "draft resister," but the term typically describes an individual who refuses to be conscripted into the military.

assemble some of the pieces of the broader mosaic, to tell a little of the story of those who have refused when ordered to train for war.

History may not provide us with a record of the first man in North America to obtain recognition as a conscientious objector. We do know that the first law allowing for CO exemption from bearing arms was enacted by the Massachusetts Bay Colony in 1661. Several colonies passed similar statutes in the following decades. These laws were intended to protect the religious liberty of Quakers, Mennonites, Brethren, and members of other Christian "peace churches," whose traditions require or strongly encourage members not to bear arms against other human beings. Not all colonies were tolerant of objectors; in 1666 Virginia set a fine of 100 pounds of tobacco for refusing to drill with the militia. Elsewhere objectors were whipped or jailed.

Fortunately, even military officers were not uniformly hostile to COs. In 1756, during the Seven Years War (also called the French and Indian War) George Washington found himself commanding a unit that had arrested seven Quaker objectors. Washington ordered the men freed.

At the time of the American Revolution, Quakers in Philadelphia who refused to enter the militia were taxed the modest sum of two pounds ten shillings per year. Congress publicly urged objectors to contribute money for "the relief of their distressed brethren," but did not require such contributions. Religious objectors were sometimes viewed as British sympathizers, but often were granted respect.

During the Civil War, partly because the national army rather than locally elected militia officers controlled the draft apparatus, conscientious objectors suffered cruelly. Laws in both North and South gave recognition to religious COs, and many were given civilian work on farms, but officers sent others into the army illegally. At military camps they were often beaten or hanged by their thumbs; some were executed.

In Virginia, Quaker Seth Laughlin was taken before a Rebel firing squad. When he prayed for the souls of his executioners, the soldiers lowered their rifles. Eventually he was freed, but not before other soldiers beat him. By war's end, about 1,200 men had expressed religious objection in North and South.

Most opposition to the draft came not from religious pacifists, but from farmers and workers whose families could not endure army wages or who saw the war as a "rich man's war" (the wealthy could buy draft exemptions). Antidraft revolts were fought in Wisconsin, Illinois, Ohio, Texas, Missouri, Alabama, and New York City, where hundreds died. Thousands of men left their homes to hide from draft officials, earning themselves the sobriquet "Skedaddlers." Some men in the Northeast skedaddled across the Canadian border for a few weeks, returning undetected. By any measure, the draft was a near failure in North and South.

In 1917, when America joined World War I and began drafting men, the government abolished some practices that had provoked resentment during the Civil War draft, such as door-to-door registration and the purchase of exemptions. Other changes intended to preempt criticism included putting civilians in control of draft boards and implementing a lottery to chose draftees. In the same period, the nation's political landscape had been transformed by the rise of labor, socialist, and women's suffrage movements. Each of these movements was divided over the question of opposing World War I, but they all furnished leaders for antiwar and antidraft struggles.

Partly due to the influence of these movements, many people began to oppose war on nonreligious grounds, arguing that war and military spending were anti-working class or that they blocked needed social reforms. Many nonreligious socialists, anarchists, and humanitarians now demanded CO status. Laws written for religious objectors did not include them, and most were imprisoned.

At the same time, many recently arrived immigrants bore grudges against America's allies in the war. Some had come to this country to escape European draft calls. A handful went to jail or fled the country. Some were tarred and feathered; a German mistakenly believed to be antiwar was hanged in Illinois. The presence of immigrants in the ranks of dissenters was used to turn public opinion against radicals and peace activists by labelling them as "alien" and pro-German.

9

During this war, peace activists developed new modes of action. The first draft counseling offices were set up, the first organizations for conscientious objectors were launched and jailed resisters began to stage strikes and fasts against mistreatment. Leaders of reform movements aided resisters behind bars and pressed for amnesty for draft resisters after the war.

By war's end over 60,000 men had declared themselves objectors and 21,000 of this group were drafted in the lottery. Most were persuaded to drop their claims after spending time in stockades, where guards beat some and chained others to the bars in a standing or kneeling position for eight hours a day. About 1,200 men were sent to do civilian service on farms, and 100 did war relief work for Quakers in France, a project that led to the formation of the American Friends Service Committee.

Nearly 500 of the COs refused to cooperate with the military. Since the military had jurisdiction over those who had been given draft notices, they were all court-martialed. Life sentences were imposed on over a quarter of these objectors; 17 were sentenced to death. None were executed, but 17 others died from beatings or suicide. Press reports of the beatings and deaths led to improved treatment of resisters; from then on, civilian courts and prisons had jurisdiction over men who refused their draft notices.

Men whose resistance began prior to their induction orders, such as nonregistrants and those who failed to report for physical examinations, were left to the civilian authorities. Over 170,000 men failed to report for physicals, about 6 percent of those who registered. The number who failed to register is impossible to determine, but was certainly in the scores of thousands. Federal law provided a maximum sentence of one year for nonregistrants, so those tried in the opening months of the war were free before the fighting stopped. Amnesty activists secured the release of the last of the objectors from military jails by 1922.

The World War II draft saw 50,000 men classed as COs. About two-thirds of them, including many Seventh Day Adventists, accepted "noncombatant" service in the military. Many served as medics, and one received the Medal of Honor for rescuing wounded men in combat. Approximately 15,000 others went to "alternate service" in civilian capacity; four-fifths of this group did reforestation, irrigation, or other work in Civilian Public Service (CPS) camps. Mental hospitals employed 2,000 with the result that neglect and abuse of patients in several states was exposed and reforms were begun. Approximately 500 volunteered for starvation diets or exposure to deadly germs in order to perfect medical treatments used for refugees and freed prisoners of war. However, about 1,000 men in CPS concluded that accepting CO status had kept them from making an effective antiwar statement. They walked out of the camps and submitted to arrest.

In CPS camps and prisons, observers noted a small number of men from two groups that had been all but absent from the ranks of resisters and objectors to the First World War: African-Americans and Catholic pacifists. Black resisters included secular pacifists and members of the Nation of Islam, a group established between the wars. Another organization founded in that period was the Catholic Worker Movement, led by Dorothy Day and Peter Maurin. Scores of men influenced by them sought CO status or chose prison. Protestants from "mainstream" churches were also more visible as objectors than in the previous war.

Prison brutality against resisters was fairly rare during World War II; the military turned custody of resisters over to civilian courts this time, and officials sought to avoid the scandals of the previous war. In the prisons, resisters inspired by the vision of Gandhi and by domestic struggles for civil rights carried out strikes and fasts against racial segregation, and won several victories. Immediately after the war, draft opponents waged an amnesty campaign for those who had been imprisoned. About one tenth of the men were given presidential pardons.

As the country demobilized from the Second World War the draft was shut down for a few months. Then, in 1948, President Truman proposed a new draft in order to challenge Soviet power. Congress quickly consented to this "emergency" measure, one that led to 25 years of draft calls.

A handful of pacifists burned their draft cards in Chicago to protest the new draft, but newspapers and prosecutors ignored this act of civil disobedience. When the draft resumed, blacks backed labor leader A. Philip Randolph in a successful campaign to desegregate the army by combining lobbying with explicit threats of an illegal "boycott" against draft registration.

By 1950, Cold War tensions were rising rapidly and Red Scare hysteria was costing radicals and alleged radicals jobs across the country. After the Korean War began that year, public opinion grew even more intolerant of dissenters. Isolated and harassed peace activists were hardly surprised to find that very few men were willing to face jail or even seek objector status during the war.

After the Korean truce in 1954, as Cold War tensions began to relax at home and abroad, CO applications mushroomed. The growth of the civil rights and ban-the-bomb movements at that time gave added impetus to the efforts of draft opponents. By the early 1960s opponents of the draft were still few in number, but were growing in sophistication and confidence. Ending the draft became a respectable, if not a majority, view; even some Republicans in Congress began calling for its repeal.

The rapid expansion of United States involvement in the Vietnam War in 1965–66 led to a leap in draft calls and the end of deferments for graduate students. By the time most American troops came home in 1973, opposition to the draft had reached levels unheard of since the Civil War.

In some ways opposition to the Vietnam draft had familiar earmarks. Most of the COs were acting from religious or moral beliefs. Long established pacifist groups like the War Resisters League and the Fellowship of Reconciliation were among the leadership.

For the most part, however, reaction to this draft was different. Ad hoc draft counseling and resistance groups sprang up in most parts of the country. An enormous underground railroad smuggled deserters and resisters to Canada. While the exact number of men who crossed the border for such purposes is impossible to know, estimates generally fall in the range of 30–60,000. Most of those who were indicted for resistance had no close ties to any religious or radical group. In fact, the lines between religious and nonreligious resistance blurred as members of peace churches, Catholics, Jews, and "mainstream" Protestants worked alongside nonreligious or politically motivated antiwar activists. Incredibly, most prosecutions against draft resisters were ultimately dropped, largely because there were not enough courts and prosecutors to try them all. Perhaps most startling was the growth of antiwar activity and groups within the armed forces; for example, over 200 antiwar newspapers were produced by GIs.

One factor that contributed to these unusual developments was the explosion of a new youth culture, especially on college campuses. The civil rights revolution, the growth of "rock and roll" culture, and alienation from materialism and conformity created a volatile mix on those campuses. A draft system that "channelled" men into college by deferring them until graduation fanned the flames of discontent.

On campus and off, the inequities in draft policies fueled anger; blacks were excluded from draft boards in many states and draft protesters often found their deferments cancelled. The Supreme Court eventually ruled against the targeting of protesters in *Gutknecht v. U.S.* (1970). The Supreme Court also overturned the conviction of the most famous black draft resister, boxer Mohammed Ali.

Two other court rulings in *U.S v. Seegar* (1965) and *Welsh v. U.S.* (1970) removed most barriers to conscientious objector status for nonreligious applicants. The rulings removed earlier requirements that the applicant claim a "traditional" religious affiliation and a belief in a Supreme Being. This change, together with widespread disillusionment with the war, encouraged hundreds of thousands of men to seek CO classification. Those who were not opposed to all war ("selective objectors") were still not eligible, and often went to prison. Others went underground, and some joined the exodus to Canada.

During the war, peace groups in the United States joined exiles in Canada in calling for amnesty for jailed resisters, exiles, and GIs who had received less-than-honorable discharges. In 1972, Democratic Presidential nominee George McGovern endorsed amnesty, a move that was fiercely criticized by veterans groups and conservatives within his own party. By 1976, the war's end (and President Ford's proclama-

I REFUSE

tion of a token "earned" amnesty for men willing to do public service work) made amnesty a less divisive issue. Draft exile Fritz Efaw addressed the Democratic National Convention together with disabled Vietnam veteran Ron Kovic. Candidate Jimmy Carter endorsed a broad amnesty for civilian draft violators, and implemented it after taking office. However, Carter did not upgrade the less-than-honorable discharges that hobbled the job searches of hundreds of thousands of veterans punished for antiwar or antiracist activity, or for "apolitical" acts of in-service defiance.

In 1980, seven years after President Nixon announced "zero draft calls," President Carter asked Congress to restore draft registration. Local and national peace groups began mobilizing protests, their sense of urgency underlined by the Soviet-Afghan war and Carter's threat to fight the Soviets if they expanded the conflict.

When registration began that summer, the National Resistance Committee, a small antimilitarist group, advocated registration refusal and publicized the statements of public nonregistrants. Long-established pacifist groups such as the War Resisters League joined new ad hoc antidraft groups in supporting nonregistrants. A new face was the Libertarian Party, a group founded in 1972 by antiauthoritarian student conservatives advocating free enterprise, civil liberty, and an end to military commitments. Draft counseling programs were established in many cities, and vigils and rallies were held opposing the new draft law.

After internal debates over ending registration, the Reagan Administration announced its continuation and soon began prosecution of a few of those men who made their resistance public. In all, 20 out of the hundreds of such men were indicted. About half were Mennonites, Brethren or Quakers. Several were anarchists, one was an anti-interventionist and two were local officers of political parties: the Socialist Party of Iowa and the Libertarian Party of Arkansas.

All the indicted political resisters and some of the religious ones welcomed protest activity opposing their prosecutions. In some cases, supporters flooded courtrooms, sit-ins were held, and hundreds of people signed "complicity statements" proclaiming their refusal to obey laws against aiding and abet-

14

INTRODUCTION

ting resisters. In these statements, which were also used in the 1960s, signers declare themselves accomplices of draft resisters and demand that the government drop charges or put the signers on trial as well.

Press coverage was often favorable to the resisters and some appeared on radio or television talk shows. Some of the resisters spent several months in minimum security prisons; others were sentenced to community service or received fines. After 1986, no new cases were brought against nonregistrants. Registration became an almost invisible issue until the Persian Gulf War.

In August 1990, a Marine corporal threw himself to the ground when Military Police tried to drag him aboard a Saudi-bound plane in Hawaii. With this act, military resistance to the Persian Gulf War began. By the time President Bush launched the war on Iraq in January 1991, several dozen women and men in the regular military forces or the reserves had publicly refused orders to deploy. Some spoke at peace rallies held in New York, Washington and other cities.

Several black, Hispanic and immigrant soldiers were among the handful of publicly known military resisters in the weeks preceding and following the launching of the Gulf War by President Bush. One African-American student in an ROTC unit refused to report for duty and was taken from his university dormitory after midnight in chains.

The military gave less than honorable discharges to a number of resisters in November and December of 1990, perhaps hoping to keep the number of CO discharges low and to avoid the publicity that would attend courts-martial. However, in January 1991, as the war began, activists perceived a trend toward rapid trials and jail sentences for military resisters.

In May 1991, two months after the cease-fire, the War Resisters League reported that about 2,500 soldiers had sought conscientious objector discharges since the crisis began, and said 150 of them were under prosecution. By August, military courts had sentenced 42 Marines to terms of 6 to 36 months in prison, and a dozen others were awaiting trial. Scores of soldiers in the other military branches were sentenced to jail as well. One of the most publicized cases was that of Army Re-

15

serve Captain Yolanda Huet-Vaughn, a physician who left her base and addressed numerous peace rallies in the weeks preceding the war. Huet-Vaughn argued in court that the government's failure to prepare to treat Iraqi civilians wounded in the war was a violation of U.S. and international law. She was found guilty of desertion in August 1991 and sentenced to 30 months in prison.

Support activities for soldiers seeking CO discharges were organized by religious pacifist groups like the American Friends Service Committee as well as secular pacifist groups. Antiwar veterans, organized in groups like Veterans for Peace and Vietnam Veterans Against the War, offered encouragement to military resisters. Draft counselors specializing in work with military personnel reported a flood of business before and during the war. Afterwards, peace activists began a campaign for amnesty for military resisters.

This story is unfinished. Women and men within the military continue to wrestle with the decision to seek conscientious objector discharges. Young men turning 18 are still required to register for the draft; those who do not are legally denied job training and student loans if discovered, and the prosecution of nonregistrants could resume whenever the Justice Department wishes. Despite the "end of the Cold War," American soldiers are involved in a war in El Salvador, in "drug wars" in South America, and on the margins of a civil war in the Philippines. It is too early to tell if the U.S. role in these wars or in the Middle East will grow.

The narrative that follows focuses on the particular details of one man's actions and experiences during the Vietnam era. I trust that those yet to face difficult decisions about war and peace will find strength in knowing what others who went before them have faced. Those decisions in some fashion confront not only soldiers and would-be soldiers, but all citizens of this nation, and all citizens of this planet. I hope this book offers some guidance, some insight and some courage to all who seek peace and the justice that makes peace possible.

—David List, Ph.D

# CHAPTER ONE
## THE COLLAPSE OF CAMELOT

The year 1967 began with United States troop strength in the Vietnam War increasing to 380,000.[1] Civilian deaths from American bombing of the North became a major controversy, but did not deter the government from gaining permission to raid from Thailand; the B-52 bombers had been flying from distant Guam. On Guam, President Lyndon Johnson met with South Vietnamese leaders, vowing to continue the war while seeking an honorable peace. Meanwhile, in Morgantown, West Virginia I studied television coverage of the war for traces of what I was taught was the humanity of Americans. Instead, I saw only more waves of destructive force pouring ashore, while men, women and children ran from flaming napalm.

Despite my suspicion that the additional troops and intensified bombing might quickly end the conflict, this escalation and the increased civilian deaths marked the beginning of my opposition to the war. Yet I was not opposed enough to be in the streets, though others were. In Europe, anti-American rallies over the war were echoed here by a new rash of marches and peace demonstrations, the largest in New York and San Francisco.[2] Flanked by prominent antiwar, civil rights, and religious leaders, Dr. Martin Luther King stepped to the podium of the New York event where he called for a halt to the bombing of North Vietnam; he had already urged a

1. *New York Times*, January 2, 1967, p. 3.
2. *New York Times*, April 16, 1967, p. 1.

17

draft boycott, saying all draft-age men should declare themselves conscientious objectors.[3]

Still, those opposing the war were not the only demonstrators that spring. New York hosted an equally inspired pro-Vietnam War rally attended by veteran groups, labor unions, and fraternal and religious organizations.[4]

Politically, President Johnson was faring well enough despite the mounting unrest. At the end of June, his popularity was at 58 percent, up from 47 percent the previous month.[5] All the while, the costs of what had become his war were rising, including 2,929 American dead and wounded in one week, a record. The 313 deaths brought the total American losses in Southeast Asia since January 1961 to over 10,000.[6] The projected financial cost of the war was approximately 26 billion dollars.[7]

These figures prompted congressional doves to become more vocal, including senators from Johnson's own party, like Mike Mansfield of Montana, and Robert Kennedy of New York. The Republican side was less vocal, although Senators Claude Aiken of Vermont, Charles Percy of Illinois, John Cooper of Kentucky, and Edward Brooke of Massachusetts were among Republicans generally identified as opposed to the war; it was Senator Aiken who gave the quickly famous quote, "We should declare victory and get out." However, as attention shifted toward the 1968 Presidential elections, Republicans like Governor George Romney called the war "tragic," and "a mistake"; their party, he said, should campaign for peace.[8]

I thought they should too; somebody should. That somebody, however, would not be from my hometown where one would not know there was a war going on; with 15,000 largely conservative townspeople, and another 15,000 similarly defined West Virginia University students, it remained business as usual. Built on the banks of the Monongahela River, Morgantown was typical of towns of the region, picturesque with tree-

3. *New York Times*, April 16, 1967, p. 2; April 5, 1967, p. 1.
4. *New York Times*, May 14, 1967, p. 1, 3.
5. *New York Times*, July 4, 1967, p. 18.
6. *New York Times*, May 26, 1967, p. 1; June 2, 1967, p. 1.
7. *New York Times*, January 25, 1967, p. 1; April 26, 1967, p. 7.
8. *New York Times*, September 5, 1967, p. 28.

thick rolling hills in all directions, broken only by the indigenous laurel and rhododendron bushes, blue violets and emerald clover in every yard.

Apart from university employees, ours was a town of factory workers, coal miners, and shopkeepers, people of generally modest means, but proud and persevering. Above all, it was a town of neighborhoods, of schools, family-run corner stores, and taverns, all reflecting the blue-collar ethic. Even the university seemed blue-collar, worker-oriented, with its strengths in agricultural and mineral sciences.

In September of 1967, I began my first year in graduate school at the university, many of us accused of continuing in school to maintain the student deferment from the draft. I had always intended graduate work, my Bachelor's degree in Psychology of little use without an advanced degree. This was not to say the prospect of renewed student deferment had no bearing whatever on my decision to remain in school; I did not want to go to Vietnam.

The safety of our largely conservative campus remained appealing in light of the increasing violence around the country over the war; indeed, in the nation's capital, an antiwar demonstration ended in a near riot at the Pentagon.[9] By contrast, in New York a counter-demonstration had people turning on their headlights in support of the government. Soon after, President Johnson responded with a speech reaffirming American commitment to remain in Vietnam as long as necessary. However, the President's support, especially among the young, was eroding; his popularity by the end of November was down to 38 percent, with any of six Republican presidential possibilities beating him in the polls.

Not helping were race riots all across the country: on July 12–17 in Newark, New Jersey, some 26 persons died, with 1,500 injured, and more than 1,000 arrested. But the single bloodiest outbreak occurred July 23–30 in Detroit, where at least 40 people died, 2,000 were injured, and 5,000 left homeless. The Detroit riot was finally quelled when President Johnson ordered 4,700 federal paratroopers to aid the 8,000 National Guardsmen already there. It was the first use of federal

9. *New York Times*, October 22, 1967, p. 1.

troops in a riot since 1943.[10] For those of us who watched on television, the appearance was that we were not only waging war against the Vietnamese, but against our own people as well.

Adding to that impression was the November 6th announcement by Defense Secretary Robert McNamara that the National Guard would be increased by 12,000 men. These would be organized into 125 company-size units which, according to National Guard sources, would include special headquarters detachments capable of coordinating emergency forces during domestic unrest.

The President's popularity among the young was further undermined by Selective Service Director Lewis B. Hershey's crackdown on student antiwar protestors who were interfering with armed forces recruiting on campuses. These students' names, Hershey said, would be moved to the top of the draft lists.[11] The protestors struck back with increased violence during "National Stop-The-Draft Week," hundreds of demonstrators were arrested in New York, Wisconsin, New Hampshire, Ohio, and Connecticut.[12]

This was not to say there was no dissent at West Virginia University. Technically it began in 1965–66 with the formation of a small antiwar group by two Quaker students. Because most on campus overwhelmingly supported the government's efforts in Vietnam, the group had difficulty finding ways to protest effectively. It was not until October 1966 that dissent at the university became realistic and acceptable. During that month a week-long, university-supported "Festival of Ideas" occurred; it featured nationally-known intellectuals who debated, among other things, the Vietnam conflict.

This festival gave the Quaker students a forum, a petition containing 80 signatures given to festival participant Vice President Hubert Humphrey. What followed though, was a counter-petition, a pro-war petition, containing 1,200 signatures collected by the campus branch of the conservative Young Americans for Freedom (YAF).

10. *New York Times*, July 14, 1967, p. 1; July 25, 1967, p. 1; August 1, 1967, p. 1.
11. *New York Times*, November 8, 1967, p. 1.
12. *New York Times*, December 5, 1967, p. 24.

Less than a month later, still in the fall of 1966, a fiery, new Episcopal chaplain polarized the campus by accusing the university administration, Festival of Ideas notwithstanding, of forcing "outmoded" bourgeois values on students and of attempting to "inoculate students with fear" and to "reinforce the docility of the student body." "This campus and this town," he proclaimed in a sermon, "need dissent, action and courageous protest. . . ."

Reading this in the local newspaper, I had a similar reaction to the majority of students and townspeople: we were being preached to by a firebrand, a transplanted Bostonian with no knowledge of the ways of West Virginians. We were quiet, respectful people who addressed our problems in a discreet, not a provocative manner. Unfortunately, concern over his style kept most from hearing the truth of his message.

In some ways, the "Festival of Ideas" debate of the Vietnam issue was West Virginia University's answer to the so-called "teach-ins" on other campuses. These began at the University of Michigan in March 1965, shortly after the first bombings of North Vietnam. For the most part, the teach-ins were an honest effort to present opposing points of view on the war, enabling participants to reach an understanding of American policy.

Michigan's teach-in was proposed and encouraged by a large number of its faculty, no less than 49 members proposed that classes be suspended for a day to permit a campus-wide exploration of the implications of American policy in the war.

While the administration agonized, campus radicals dreamed of transforming the proposal into a full-scale confrontation. Finally, however, a compromise was reached whereby the various parties agreed that public discussions of the war would begin at the end of classes one afternoon and go on, if necessary, throughout the night.

On March 24, 1965 over 3,500 students and professors crowded into four lecture halls on the Michigan campus, and discussions began. As the hours went by, teachers spoke about the war, students asked questions or argued, seminar groupings formed and reformed until at last it was dawn the next day. News of the Michigan event spread quickly through the academic world, and soon faculty/student groups elsewhere made similar arrangements. Another teach-in was held at Columbia the next night, and in following days at the University of Wisconsin, New York University, Rutgers, and the University of Oregon. Much less celebrated institutions, from Western Reserve to Flint Junior College, also enthusiastically joined in the movement. Then on May 15, a "national teach-in" was held in Washington D.C., connected by telephone to 122 campuses across the country.

While all these events, including West Virginia's 1966 Festival of Ideas, were well and good, it was not until the draft began singling out young people, that the issue became something other than intellectual debate. Actually, the spring teach-ins of 1965 seemed almost to trigger what proved a massive singling out, as in the coming months draft calls skyrocketed. For instance, the October 1965 call was for 40,200 men, the highest since the Korean war. By the following summer, all the calls were upped four to six thousand per month until in October 1966, 46,200 were inducted, well beyond any Korea draft. The elimination of such deferments as married men without children, also began at this time. President Kennedy had ceased their call in 1963, President Johnson resuming it in 1965.

My singling out began on November 30, 1967 with a letter from my local draft board asking for verification of my graduate status; I could do this by filling out a form at the graduate school. Thinking little of it, I sent the form back only to find I was now classified I-A, available for service. I was stunned. Had I been mistaken for a protestor interfering with recruiters; why was my name now at the top of the draft list? As I thought about it though, it made more sense; the local board had meant to draft me with the end of my undergraduate deferment, when I graduated in May. They were attempting to cover their oversight with this I-A reclassification, despite my being a full-time graduate student, in good standing.

That the university should have something to say about this prompted me to ask the department chairman to inquire of the local board their grounds for the I-A. This he did, and together we waited anxiously for the reply which, for all I knew, might come in the form of an induction order.

That I was preoccupied by the turn of events was an understatement. Until this time I had avoided thinking about the draft, a response not uncommon to young men of my generation. Born at the end of World War II, we grew up in the peaceful 1950s and early 1960s when draft calls were small and deferments plentiful. During the Kennedy Administration, for example, some monthly drafts were zero. As for those who were inducted, they had only peacetime duty facing them.

For many of us, when it came time for college there was no question of enrolling; we had always been, and planned to continue being students. There was no reason not to continue. If I was upset and angered by the draft board's intrusion, it was because I now had to take a stand on the war; it was no longer enough to say I opposed the war's escalation, or the bombing of civilians in the North.

In point of fact, my feelings about Vietnam had been intensifying, though the shape of these was another matter; they were a blend of conflicts. On the one hand, there was patriotism, and on the other, morality; I did not expect them to be different things. It seemed to me patriotism was why most went to Vietnam. I doubted they were there because they thought they were doing what was morally right. While I considered myself as patriotic as the next guy, my feelings regarding the morality of the war were stronger.

Resisting the draft became an option when I heard Dr. Benjamin Spock at a press conference. He and four others had just been indicted "for conspiring to abet, aid and counsel violators of the Selective Service Act." He said resisting the draft was "a very patriotic endeavor . . . the most effective way of opposing the war." But was I that opposed? Failing to comply with a draft order was a federal offense. Was I prepared to go to prison over my opposition?

Greatly affecting my thinking at the time was a letter I sent to a friend, one of many personal letters I sent to high school friends who had gone into the military, most seeing duty in Vietnam. I did not know this individual was in the war until I read a local newspaper article saying he had been wounded.

We had known each other off and on, dating back to Little League baseball. While I attended one of the public high schools, he was enrolled in the area Catholic high school where he was a star athlete, President of the Student Council, and a member of the Honor Society. We became closer during a psychology course at the university, where I came to appreciate his intelligence and good humor. I wrote in the letter:

> I read in the paper today where you had some bad luck. I thought I would drop you a line to let you know I am one of the home folks pulling for you. I sincerely hope your injury isn't a severe one. . . .

Eventually, the letter was returned to me with rubber stamps all over it, the last one reading "Verified Deceased." The sting of that left me speechless, as suddenly what had been a television war struck home.

But there was more to it than that for me. This was not simply a "reality sandwich," as one of my professors put it. Certainly the realization that I would never again see my friend, hurt; but such emotion would be overcome in time, with grieving, as I now grieved. What could not be overcome was that his death was wrong. And by that I was not referring to the political issues of the war, but to something much deeper and much more human. This event marked the beginning of the end of my cooperation with the system.

About the same time, President Johnson stated that he did not think the North Vietnamese were any more ready to negotiate than they had been over the past two years. Recent American peace probes, he noted, had gone "as far as honorable men could go." Then in Dallas he announced, "There must be no weakening of will that would encourage the enemy and prolong the bloody conflict." He continued that American and South Vietnamese forces had "answered aggression's onslaught with one strong voice, declaring, 'No retreat'." "That must be our answer, too, here at home. No retreat from responsibility. . . ."

With that, the government eliminated all graduate school deferments. I was ordered for a preinduction physical examination.

Failing the physical exam was how many were exempted from military service, the slightest suggestion of a limiting ailment inviting the family doctor to write a letter to the draft board. This began happening so frequently that local boards soon required second opinions.

During 1967, 125,000 men were rejected based on medical information provided prior to preinduction physical exams. Of those sent for the physical exams, 400,000 men (37 percent) were found unacceptable, about two-thirds for medical reasons, and the rest for mental or administrative reasons, like drug use or criminal offenses.[13]

It is not possible to determine how many men successfully fooled the system, but stories of attempts, and how to do it, became part of the Sixties culture. The most famous examples were Arlo Guthrie's classic folk song, *Alice's Restaurant* and the book, *1001 Ways to Beat the Draft*.

I was not surprised that these attempts began to increase, even in the conservative state of West Virginia. Indeed, I knew some people who tried to become medically disqualified on their own. Starting two days prior to the exam, an acquaintance of mine stayed up all night drinking alcohol and smoking cigarettes, then stayed up all day drinking coffee and smoking cigarettes. He did not shave or bathe or brush his teeth, so that when he went in for the exam, he was so repulsive, and his blood pressure was so high, he was immediately given a IV-F disqualification. (Of the 15 Selective Service deferment and exemptions classifications, the IV-F was for those unfit for physical, mental, or administrative reasons.) It was only after others in the area began doing this that the medical staff at the induction center began holding them over for 24 hours to see if their condition improved, which it usually did.

My self-respect denied me this option. Instead, I rode with the other prospective inductees to the examination center. I knew several on the bus from high school, all of us losing graduate school deferments.

I have never been more embarrassed or humiliated than I was during that government-ordered physical examination. Still, I was able to put it into a frame of reference just to get

13. Arlo Tatum and Joseph S. Tuchinsky, *Guide to the Draft* (Boston: Beacon Press, 1969), pp. 170, 180.

through it: I pretended it was a school gym class, just us guys. Yet it remained offensive, as in what I called the "get on your mark, get set, urinate" segment. No bathroom had seen so many young men at one time, each struggling in his way to produce the required quantity of urine in the test tube provided. The lucky ones knew the successful guy next to him, and could "borrow" some.

To this embarrassment was added the anal exam, whereby 10 men at a time lined up, dropped their pants and spread their buttocks. Completely degrading, it reduced us to livestock. The younger ones giggled, a sign of their embarrassment; however, the rest of us just gritted our teeth, swearing under our breaths.

I found being ordered around by strangers who seemed to resent us to be completely depressing; everything I had been striving for in my life, self-sufficiency and independent thinking, was now threatened. It was an assault on my psychology that I had not quite anticipated.

Two hours later, after enduring the ordeal of mass physical examination, we departed by the same bus. For some it had been good news, the smiles on their faces confirming they had failed. The rest of us though, maintained our frowns, resigned now to the inevitability of induction.

"Vietnam here we come," joked one young fellow on the bus. The war would be derring-do for him, was the tone of it, which upset me all the more. The fact was, for some, especially those just out of high school, Vietnam seemed like an adventure. For others, meanwhile, it would be the solution to their problems of unemployment, or low self-esteem, although I was sure that most were hoping for solutions other than going into the army; but they felt powerless in the face of the government. At that moment, so did I.

"What are you going to do?" asked a friend next to me, the tension in my body giving me away.

Mostly he seemed surprised to see me there at all; I did not know where else he thought I would be. Already drafted maybe. Then again, I was also surprised to see him there with the others. It dawned on me that what we were feeling was the reality of the war coming home; it was there with us in that very bus. This was not how we were accustomed to seeing or relating to each other, that is, in an army bus as prospective soldiers for a foreign war. That many of us were in graduate school, made it feel even more incredible.

"What are *you* going to do?" I asked, turning the tables.

"Go in and take my chances I guess," he said finally, remorsefully.

"I should have said I was gay," joked somebody else.

"What does that have to do with it?" I said, though I knew what he meant; homosexuality was grounds for disqualification in the IV-F category. I could only imagine how embarrassing it was, what an invasion of privacy for true homosexuals faced with the draft; no doubt many went in just to protect their private lives.

Naturally these developments with the draft greatly concerned my family, their reactions being a product of their life experiences. My father was an educator, a Ph.D in chemical engineering, a political moderate, a believer in traditional values, a Lion's Club member, scout master, Junior Deputies (youth club) organizer, civil defense instructor; a pilot in the Naval Reserves, he retired as a captain.

At the time he did not express himself on the prospect of my being drafted, but his body language and facial expressions indicated he was concerned; he wanted me to be able to continue in school. With my father though, often what was not said was more revealing than what was.

For example, I was sure he had definite feelings about "duty to the country," but he did not talk about that or otherwise give me a lecture on the responsibilities of citizenship; he knew I understood that already. Rather, his position seemed to be that the decision was mine; indeed, since I turned 18 his policy had been for me to make my own decisions, for better or worse. Still, he could see how I was struggling with this one.

While my father was from Ohio, my homemaker mother was born and raised more clearly in the Midwest, in conservative Wisconsin. A Pollyanna in her way, her attitude toward my draft decision was that, while she was concerned, " . . . everything will work out all right," and "for the best," whatever that meant. It was, in fact, a mixed signal because I knew she was conservative and from a tradition where men went into the military when called, as her brother had during

World War II. So despite her expressing concern for me, like my father in mostly nonverbal ways, I sensed she preferred I yield to the draft; unlike my father, when she said "Let's wait and see," it seemed a hope I would change my mind regarding any thoughts of resisting; mostly she favored that I not draw attention to myself, hence the family, by being different.

As for my brother, older by three years, he was married with two dependent children and as such held what was known as a III-A deferment. In this way, the draft was not an issue for him, "I hope you don't have to go," being the extent of his feelings on it. The idea of *not* going, of resisting, did not seem to occur to him, anymore than it initially occurred to my parents. Actually, my parents had a better sense of how important this was becoming to me, as I was still living at home while attending college, and they got a daily picture. But for all intents and purposes, my brother was my father on this, including the inclination to not say much of anything, to wait and see.

As a result, I felt completely isolated. Inspiration had to come from elsewhere, as when I read that the American Civil Liberties Union (ACLU), long a champion of human rights in the courts, had reversed its position and agreed to defend persons accused of counseling evasion of the draft. Also inspiring was a report from Clovis, New Mexico: Air Force Captain Dale E. Noyd was convicted of disobeying an order to train pilots for Vietnam duty; a twelve-year veteran, he said he conscientiously opposed the war. He had previously attempted to resign his commission, but the Air Force refused to accept it, and sentenced him to a year at hard labor and dismissal from the service. There was also the case of Army Captain Howard Brett Levy, who in Fort Jackson, South Carolina was court-martialed for refusing to teach medicine to Green Beret corpsmen destined to fight in Vietnam. The court-martial heard another doctor, Captain Ivan Mauer say he too would refuse to give such instruction.

Meanwhile in Vietnam, a five-nation allied force of 100,000 men launched the largest drive of the war to clear Communist forces in the 11 provinces around Saigon. Elsewhere in the war, 10 American helicopters were shot down by anti-aircraft, while to the North, United States planes carried out another

155 raids. Back home, a major call-up of reservists to active duty affected 24,000 Army, Air Force, and Navy men. Secretary of Defense Clark Clifford subsequently announced a new in-country troop ceiling of 549,000.

This came on the heels of the surprise announcement by President Johnson that "I shall not seek, and I will not accept the nomination of my party for another term as your President." No doubt contributing to his decision was the strength shown in the New Hampshire primary of antiwar-Senator Eugene McCarthy, and the subsequent entry of fellow democrat, Senator Robert Kennedy. On the Republican side, another surprise was the pullout of war opponent George Romney and of Governor Nelson Rockefeller, leaving only Richard Nixon an active candidate. Rockefeller, however, came back in on learning of Johnson's decision; Democratic Vice President Hubert Humphrey also finally declared himself a candidate.

The presidential race was destined to be overshadowed by the 1968 assassination of Martin Luther King; riots broke out in Washington, Baltimore, and Chicago. Dr. King's involvement in the antiwar movement began in 1965 with debates within the Student Nonviolent Coordinating Committee (SNCC), the aggressive civil rights organization headed by Stokely Carmichael. SNCC's Third World orientation brought it inevitably to the conclusion that Vietnam was a colonial war, waged by whites against people of color, like themselves.

Still, neither King nor black liberals were yet prepared to oppose the war. While they disliked it, they were reluctant to break with Lyndon Johnson, their patron on domestic political issues. Equally important, neither wanted to precipitate a schism in the civil rights movement by openly attacking SNCC.

Then in 1966, a group of SNCC members picketed the Atlanta induction center where all were arrested. Six were sentenced to serve three-and-a-half years for "interfering with the administration of the Selective Service Act."[14] Another picketer was sentenced to three years for "insurrection." If

14. Stephen M. Kohn, *Jailed for Peace: The History of American Draft Law Violators, 1658–1985* (Westport, Connecticut: Greenwood Press, 1986), p. 80.

this seemed severe, it only underscored other injustices blacks experienced at home with the draft and in the war.

In *Jailed for Peace: The History of American Draft Law Violators, 1658–1985,* Stephen M. Kohn documented that minorities were systematically under-represented on draft boards. At one time, 23 states did not have a single black board member, despite blacks being over-represented in the armed services. To begin with, they were drafted at a rate almost twice as high as whites, with people from low-income backgrounds generally twice as likely to see combat duty in Vietnam than people from middle or high-income families.

Kohn added that legal attempts to end discrimination in the racial composition of draft boards failed, as in the case of Cleveland C. Sellers, a founder and national officer of SNCC indicted for draft resistance. Sellers challenged the legality of his induction order issued by an all-white draft board. A military psychiatrist chastised Sellers, calling him a "semi-professional race agitator." Sellers' challenge was subsequently rejected by the trial court and he received the maximum sentence of five years in prison. The Supreme Court then refused to hear Sellers' appeal and affirmed his conviction.

In another draft case described by Kohn, a black defendant claimed that the chairman of his local all-white draft board was a member of the Ku Klux Klan. At his trial the court refused to allow questioning of the chairman concerning the alleged KKK membership; the youth was convicted and sentenced to five years in prison.

These sorts of injustices contributed to Dr. King's eventual opposition to the war. When he did though, it was not without opposition by other blacks. Roy Wilkins of the National Association for the Advancement of Colored People (NAACP), for example, vigorously opposed King on the grounds that the cause of civil rights should remain divorced from foreign policy. But after painful self-examination King concluded that at the very least his personal commitment to nonviolence must include the Vietnam War, even if it meant burning his bridges to Lyndon Johnson, and to some within the civil rights movement. So, on March 25, 1967 he led his first antiwar demonstration in Chicago, where he called on "all those who love peace" to "combine the fervor of the civil rights movement with the peace movement."

It was shortly thereafter, in a speech at New York City's Riverside Church that he made his position abundantly clear. Speaking to a crowd of over 3,000 King said,

> . . . We have been faced with the irony of watching Negro and white boys on TV screens as they kill and die together for a nation that has been unable to seat them together in the same schools. So we watch them in brutal solidarity burning the huts of a poor village, but we realize they would never live on the same block in Detroit.

King then declared, "I knew that I could never again raise my voice against the violence of the oppressed in the ghettos without having first spoken clearly to the greatest purveyor of violence in the world today—my own government."[15]

Then, in April 1967, King participated in one of the largest antiwar demonstrations to date in New York. At this demonstration 150 men burned their draft cards at dawn in Central Park. Participants then marched to the United Nations Plaza led by Dr. King, Dr. Benjamin Spock, Reverend James Bevel, and other prominent figures, arms linked in solidarity.[16] But King's involvement in the antiwar movement was destined to last less than a year, a sniper's bullet taking his life.

And the violence continued, especially on the nation's campuses. Columbia University saw a major upheaval marked by bloody clashes with police, the campus all but paralyzed for two weeks. Other universities experiencing student turmoil over a wide range of issues were the University of Maryland, Cornell University, University of Chicago, Cheyne State College, Roosevelt University, and Southern Illinois University, among others.[17]

---

15. Lionel Lokos, *House Divided: The Life and Legacy of Martin Luther King* (New Rochelle, New York: Arlington House, 1968), p. 380.

16. Lokos, pp. 376, 390; Milton Viorst, *Fire in the Streets: America in the 1960s* (New York: Simon and Schuster, 1979), p. 405.

17. Viorst, p. 441.

On the campus of West Virginia University where I continued my first year graduate studies with the shadow of the draft over me, there were no major student protests. Mostly we were abuzz about Johnson's decision not to run again, big news in a traditionally Democratic state. Many of us were jubilant; could the war and the draft be about to end? Fueling our hopes was President Johnson's subsequent announcement that formal peace talks would begin with North Vietnam on May 12, 1968 in Paris.

As it happened, I now had a different circle of friends. As an undergraduate, I maintained a few more or less close student friends, and a handful of student acquaintances, our gathering regularly for beer and conversation, usually about classes or the upcoming football game. However, in graduate school I became close to a fellow graduate student in our department whom I will call Mac. In many ways it seemed an unlikely friendship, as I was more conservative in politics, appearance, and mannerisms.

Three years older than me, shorter and stockier, he had thick black hair, with a beard at the mouth from which frequently hung a cigarette. Also, it was not uncommon to see him dressed menacingly, rapping through town on his "chopper" motorcycle. In fact, it was this same machine which he frequently rebuilt in the kitchen of his marijuana and alcohol reeking apartment. But if people unfamiliar with him cut a wide path when he entered the room, the rest of us made a narrow path to be around him. Gregarious and good humored, he was a favorite friend.

As for our attraction to each other, it was more my being drawn to him than the other way around; I admired and envied his Bohemian lifestyle, and his "doing his own thing," as did others. But I would say the root of our friendship was the knowledge that we could never be each other.

Mac knew early on about my problems with the draft, although I expected little sympathy, knowing he was an ex-Marine. Even so, in the coming months it became apparent that my increasing doubts about the war were his doubts too.

A tavern called the Washington Cafe had become our social center. Long hair was prevalent here before it was common, with drugs of various kinds, still a novelty, available for the asking. Mostly we were students, though a few townspeople representing the original clientele, remained. In fact, at times it looked quite bizarre, with the local police fraternizing with the hippies.

Perhaps the most peculiar of all was the relationship between the owner-operator of the Cafe, and his shaggy new clientele. A simple, God-fearing Catholic, conservative to the core, no one was more amazed than him at how his spare little business was suddenly prospering. Yet one had the impression that given a choice, he would rather have the turnabout by any other means than a room full of hippies. On the other hand, he was not about to bite the hand that fed him, albeit when he went to morning mass, as he did every morning, I suspected his prayers of gratitude were followed by "why me?"

The Washington Cafe was a single, rectangular room with a high ceiling and two rotating fans. Several darkly varnished booths hugged either long wall, while two pedestalled metal tables sat in the middle. Otherwise, there were stools around an L-shaped bar, actually the top of the coolers, and another small stand-up bar near the front door.

Indirect lighting came from the neon in the front window, one pinball machine, the jukebox, the television, a few lamps here and there, but not a lot else. The real atmosphere, the personality of the place, came from quaint habits of the owner-operator—like storing every conceivable salable snack and sundry item in gallon jars, recycled pickled pigs feet jars. There was something obsessive-compulsive about it, the vessels were everywhere, as were votive candles, for sale of course. Then there were those plastic plants. . . .

Only a handful of us could truly be called regulars at the Cafe, those of the late night time slot, 10 p.m. until closing at 1 a.m. If I could be said to have a support group during the early months of my draft problems, it would include these people.

This was not to say their support of my questioning the war and the draft necessarily made sense—again Mac was an ex-Marine, another was in the Army Reserves, several had IV-F medical disqualifications—all potentially individuals who could care less.

33

Eventually, I asked Mac how a former Marine could oppose the war. "I went into the Corps when I was 16 years old," he said. "That was 1959. I had just finished my junior year in high school, where I was more or less a medium grade juvenile delinquent."

"I didn't know the military took sixteen-year-olds," I said.

"My parents had to sign. Anyway, they, the school principal, our priest, and the police all agreed six months of Marine Corps training was the prescription for me."

"You needed discipline?"

"Something like that," said Mac with a grin. "But hey, it was a neat deal to a sixteen-year-old. Six months active duty; no war going on; a dress blue, Marine uniform; and besides, in my youth culture it was okay. Macho, and all that."

"So when did you see things differently?"

"I started Fairmont State College here in West Virginia in 1961. We were increasing the number of 'military advisors' in Vietnam during those years, advisors who were really troop leaders out in the field. That was when the peace movement began."

"And you got involved?"

"I was becoming more and more iconoclastic, so that my early involvement in the peace movement was at least in part an anti-establishment gesture. And I had credibility. Because I was still in the Marine Corps, my opinion meant something. As the sixties have gone along, my antiwar feelings have grown, so that now I see the war as nothing less than a senseless and tragic manipulation of American youth."

Hence Mac's "scolding/ribbing" of the reservist who, from time to time, had to go to camp. "You should be ashamed of yourself," he would say. "Why don't you go full time, go over to the war. That's what you're trained for."

The fact was, the reservist did feel guilty about being in the military at that time, bearing in mind that like Mac, there was no war when he enlisted either. Meanwhile, understanding the peace point of view, via the Cafe, he was opposed to the war to the extent he could be; clearly though, he felt in a bind. As for what would happen if his company was ordered to Vietnam, I doubted he would disobey. Nor did I think he would resist from within the military; he had not so far. Then again, he was a prime example of how the war was now doubted on the grass roots level, by both civilians and citizen-soldiers. Other resisters in our town also had support groups. One young man, vulnerable because of a draft call, was so influenced by student activists I wondered whether they got him into more trouble than he might otherwise have seen. Then again, before it was all over the same would be thought of me.

But if some of us were new moderates, and others "radicals," there were also those who compromised with the Selective Service by applying for conscientious objector status and going into the military as noncombatants. Seventh Day Adventists were in this group, although their ranks also included Catholics, Jews, and men from other Protestant denominations. These were individuals for whom duty and conscience were equally powerful forces, resulting in considerable suffering when faced with an induction order. Ultimately, they chose noncombatant status in an attempt to render to both Caesar and to God. Of course, the draft boards liked them because despite being noncombatants they could still be used to fill induction quotas. The only problem was they usually became medics, and as unarmed members of the command structure, they often tended to wind up "Verified Deceased."

Death though was in the air in 1968, Martin Luther King's assassination soon followed by Robert Kennedy's; the antiwar movement had begun its own casualty count.

# CHAPTER TWO
## WINDING ROAD TO COURAGE

At the Democratic National Convention in August 1968, Chicago police beat young antiwar demonstrators who felt they had been abandoned by the political system. They were right. The convention nominated Hubert Humphrey, Richard Nixon having been nominated by the Republicans earlier that month. All the while, the Paris peace talks were accomplishing nothing as President Johnson washed his hands proclaiming it was "up to Hanoi now." America would not de-escalate until Hanoi indicated it would make a serious move toward peace.

As the summer of 1968 came to a close I still had not received an order to report for induction. Had the local board forgotten me again? I proceeded to enroll and began my second year of graduate work. No sooner had I done so, however, than the department chairman received a letter from the local board acknowledging his original inquiry; they confirmed that all graduate deferments, including mine, had been eliminated, which was to say I was still considered available for service. The department chairman responded with a letter stating I was in my second year, and was an experienced and valued graduate assistant whom he could not readily replace on short notice; would they consider postponing my induction until after the current school year?

Several weeks passed until another letter came saying my file had been reviewed, and as I was already enrolled they would postpone as requested. Actually, doing this was illegal and would have bearing later in my case; but for now I was beside myself with relief, it gave me more time to decide my position.

Moreover, there were signs that the war might soon end. Both Humphrey and Nixon were emphasizing the importance of peace in Southeast Asia. Also, President Johnson, in a last ditch effort to salvage his image for posterity, ordered a halt to all American aerial, naval, and artillery bombardment of the North; he then announced that the peace talks would be broadened.

That I had been given a reprieve was especially welcome from the standpoint of choosing my final course of action. It was one thing to ride out the war on a postponement, but what if in the end I did get the induction order? Would I resist? And if I did resist, would it be for the right reasons? That I resented being ordered around by military types was not enough; again, refusing induction was a felony. Even burning one's draft card brought heavy penalties, as seen in New England where two young men were tried and sentenced to prison for burning their cards, one getting five years.[18]

So what options did I have if finally, induction notice in hand, I decided to resist? I imagined I could go "underground," disappearing somewhere in the country for six years, or until the statute of limitations for criminal prosecution ran out. I subsequently heard that the statute did not apply to draft law violators. Canada and Sweden were possibilities, but included the prospect of never again setting foot on American soil. Then there was prison. I could go and tough it out, the maximum sentence of served time being five years, though the average was 33 to 36 months. All in all, not great choices. That left complying with the induction order, the simplest and easiest thing to do, as it was meant to be.

As I thought about it though, going "underground" seemed not a bad choice. That the statute of limitations excluded draft offenders did not rule out a future amnesty permitting a resurfacing. And there were advantages, like familiarity with the home culture, not having to go through an immigration process, and the availability of a seemingly endless variety of places in which to lose oneself. I had driven across the country

18. *U.S. v. O'Brien*, 391 U.S. 362 1968 (1969).

the previous year, and knew of scores of locations I would never be found. Finally, for what it was worth, there was the adventure of it, not completely unappealing to a young man.

However, the reason going underground could not be an option was summed up in the word, "family." My father, mother and brother would suffer more than I would, though certainly as time went on, I would suffer enough. That was to say, I would know how I was faring minute by minute, day by day, while all they could do was worry. Communication would be possible, but at great risk; I would have to assume their phone was tapped, the mail intercepted, and family movement monitored. Still, I could get messages in and out if it were planned carefully, though face-to-face meetings would be out of the question. Certainly I would be living in constant paranoia, which would take its toll.

In Canada and Sweden the violation of American draft law was not an extraditable offense, making exile a very real option. Historically, Canada had an open door immigration policy, and Sweden was politically and socially liberal. England would be a choice were it not nearly impossible to get admitted as an immigrant. As for going south of the border, many Latin American countries were legally bound to extradite draft law offenders, though few actually did. Initially, I was unaware of some of these details, but became so with the publication of Tatum and Tuchinsky's *Guide to the Draft*.

Then there was prison. In one way, this was the best choice, it seemed to satisfy both duty and conscience. I could fulfill my mounting sense of duty to the antiwar movement; at the same time my conscience could rest knowing I was legally beyond participation in the war. Still, once in, how soon before I was forgotten? And, what of the strain on my family, to say nothing of the strain on myself in face of the dangers of prison?

On the other hand, was there not a long history, a tradition in America of resistance to conscription and war by going to prison? Especially during World Wars I and II, pacifists often went to prison rather than go to war. Of them it was written,

Pacifists in jail are political prisoners, not ordinary criminals. They have courted imprisonment to prove the strength of their convictions, to testify to the truth as

39

they see it, to try to win public opinion, and to try to persuade the government by their voluntary suffering.[19]

And they did suffer. For example, during World War I men who resisted all military authority, called "absolutists," endured horrendous treatment in prison. *In Jailed for Peace*, Kohn gives the examples of Robert Cage, Philip Grosser, Julius Firestone, and Ernest Gellert who were respectively, beaten, nearly hanged to death, tarred and feathered, and driven to suicide.

Despite this harsh treatment, World War II saw even more conscientious objectors and resisters in prison. These men even organized themselves and staged work strikes for improved conditions and civil rights for prisoners. A debt of gratitude is owed them not just for prison reform, but for subsequent laws securing alternative civilian service for conscientious objectors.

Martin Luther King was frequently incarcerated as part of his "active nonviolent resistance." In his essay "Pilgrimage to Nonviolence," he wrote that the nonviolent resister "does not seek to dodge jail. If going to jail is necessary, he enters it ' . . . as a bridegroom enters the bride's chamber.'" No, going to prison could be a noble thing.

Even though my mind spelled out and analyzed these options I could not hide my disbelief over being in this situation at all. It was not how life was supposed to go, as far back as my first speculating about it. Ironically, back then if asked what I would be when I grew up I might have said, "a soldier," what with the influence of war movies and war toys.

Like other kids in the 1950s, I played with war toys; that was predominantly what was on the market. I assembled model warplanes made of wood or plastic and played with toy machine guns, tanks, and artillery. We imitated what we saw at the movies, especially the newsreels which showed battle footage from World War II and Korea.

I felt fine playing with these kinds of toys, seeing who could "die the best" when machine-gunned while running across the

19. Staughton Lynd and Michael Ferber, *The Resistance* (Boston: Beacon Press, 1971), p. 289.

backyard. It was fun. How could I feel differently? It was only play. Besides, it was the norm, given our militarized society at the close of World War II; why not be like a soldier? Were they not heroes?

Having said that, if I were pressed to reveal what I really wanted to be, I would have said "a minister." That was because I was baptized at age nine by a minister I thought was the greatest man in the whole world. I sang in his choir, attended Sunday school and church service each week, and went to Vacation Bible School in the summer.

However, by age 13 my interest in religion slipped into the background as hormones and issues of self-identity moved to the forefront. But by 15, I found renewed interest in religion and at 17 was one of three "speakers of the gospel" at the high school Senior Sermon the night before our graduation.

This was not to say I was a model Christian; I also learned to smoke cigarettes, drink beer and swear, we all did. It made us feel like adults.

At age 17, the idea of soldiering reappeared, and I applied for admission to the United States Naval Academy. As it happened, I was relieved when I learned I missed getting in, finishing a "Second Alternate." In fact, the only reason I attempted it was to please my father, who was ex-Navy.

Actually, my father never tried to influence me one way or the other about the military. As for this particular episode, it turned out he was proud of me anyway. "How many young people have such an experience?" he said. He was referring to my correspondence, and face-to-face meetings with West Virginia congressmen, senators, and senior officers in the Department of Navy and the Naval Reserve; it was all part of getting support for one's application to an Academy.

However, what was finally evidenced was not so much my interest in the military, as a desire to be taken seriously when I said I was going to do something; once I started a thing, I wanted the reputation of finishing it.

Still, as I left high school I was absolutely convinced that interest in the military and being religious was not in the least contradictory. Soldiers went to church; churches had special services honoring soldiers and veterans. And were there not "military chaplains?"

In the fall of 1968, a lull in ground fighting that followed the halt of American bombing of the North was replaced by intensified combat in the demilitarized zone. In the meantime, following a shaky start, the expanded Paris peace talks finally got underway. Here at home it was now *President* Richard Nixon, his winning a close election over Hubert Humphrey. I had written-in Eugene McCarthy; but I accepted Nixon because it seemed that the Republicans were now in the ideal political position to end the war.

If there was hope in the air, it was reflected by the release of Captain Lloyd Bucher, and the 82 surviving crew members of the intelligence ship *Pueblo*. They had been seized 11 months earlier by four North Korean patrol boats for allegedly violating its 12-mile territorial limit. Also, in time for Christmas, Americans were treated to the flight around the moon by the *Apollo Eight* astronauts. Back on earth, however, the Paris peace talks were stalled over the shape of the table.

Christmas 1968 was trying for me. I continued to struggle with what to do when an induction notice came. I continually asked myself questions and questioned my motives. Why was the draft a problem for me? Was I genuinely opposed to the war and fighting, or was it the threat posed to my personal freedom? Perhaps it had to do with how I was raised; had my parents instilled a sense of independence in me? Or was I insecure, always needing to be in control? Being in the army was the opposite to my being in control. Analyze as I might, I concluded it was something else. It had to do with what I had been taught, my training, values and religion.

For instance, my parents taught that it was always better to give than to receive, my father exemplifying it as a career educator, and my mother as a hospital volunteer. Their efforts were not in selfish pursuits, but in helping others in whatever ways they could.

Words or acts of hostility never came from them; I could not imagine either of them, especially my father, being violent. In this way, both stressed the importance of education, for it was through education and a well-trained mind that we lived without violence; through education we learned negotiation, compromise and respect for differing points of view.

Then there were values set by early religious training. The emphasis was on love and compassion for others. Life was a gift we were to nurture in harmony with all God's creations. The opposite was war, prime example of the sin of pride, where we believed ourselves in charge of life. In this way we prohibited the love of God from working through us. Love was the goal of life, not the failing of war.

I could not understand, however, why this view seemed to be held by a minority in a town where it was taught to so many. Why was everyone else choosing war? I did not know, but it did make me feel lonely. Either there was something right with me—I had gotten the message—or there was something wrong with them.

For all their good qualities, even my parents hedged on the issue of war. My mother would simply describe how things were in her hometown of Milwaukee, Wisconsin during World War II, and how her brother had served in the army. "Those were very patriotic times," she said, "lots of parades and flag-waving. And those who served in the army, well, they certainly were looked up to. In fact, young men seen on the streets during the war were made to feel guilty for not being in. I would hate for you to have to experience anything like that."

Because she was raised a Christian Scientist, I thought she would have a sense of the moral issues of Vietnam, or war generally, including World War II. Instead, her concern was that I not be different.

As for my Episcopalian-raised father, being a university professor made him more inclined to see war as a complex issue. Even so, when push came to shove I knew he was every bit the traditionalist my mother was. So we did not discuss war, which frankly he seemed relieved about. "This is something you have to decide for yourself," he said.

Meanwhile, in January 1969 my father brought me a note sent to his office at the university. It was from one of his graduates who had learned I was struggling with the war. The note read:

It takes courage to make a strong affirmation for life, at a time when people still believe that the way to peace is by killing. A. J. Muste said, "There is no way to peace. Peace is the way."

I was genuinely touched and inspired by this message, coming unexpectedly as it did. The problem was, I did not know yet if I had the "courage to make a strong affirmation for life." In fact, if the matter had to be settled right then, I doubted it. But an event the following month clinched it for me. It involved a young man, a fellow Baptist from a fine family; a personable guy, he was someone you instinctively liked. Two years younger than me, I knew him to speak to, though regrettably we did not speak often enough. Ironically, the last time I saw him was at the Cafe, although he was not a regular there. We did, however, share such common experiences as being on the same little league baseball team, albeit at different times, and being members of the First Baptist Church; we were also in the high school band together. As it happened, when called by the draft he declared himself a conscientious objector. His choice though, was to go in as a noncombatant, to be trained as a medic.

During his time in the army he wrote his family often, and he sent audio tapes describing his experiences and feelings. The letters would later be recorded on microfilm for the West Virginia Collection, archives at the university. I read them all and I was moved by them. His words give a sense of him:

They showed a movie [in training camp] called 'Medicine in Vietnam.' It's a detailed, graphic portrayal of what's going on now medically in 'Nam—in color—living color (or perhaps dying is a better description). I can't understate its impact on me. It may have started me down the path to being a surgeon.

. . . If only those guys didn't have to return to fighting when they're fixed. If only all that medical knowledge and ability could be used to tame just nature's ills and natural accidents, instead of man-made, intentional maiming.

That's what I might like to do—gain the ability to save lives—in hopes they might learn to live in PEACE. [October 12, 1968].

. . . If I am called to 'Nam, I will go. Out of obligation to a country I love, I will go, and possibly die for a cause I vehemently disagree with.

Is any cause worth the loss of 150,000 men, women and children over the years? There may be. I don't know. But I do know now that I don't think that what's happening in 'Nam will win any cause worth 150,000 human lives. [November 1, 1968].

Does a man lose all perspective in battle? Is it possible to fight sincerely for peace? I HATE WAR!

. . . As I knelt last night at the alter rail, before me were both an American flag and a cross. Can a man kneel with integrity before both? [November 11, 1968].

Soon after, this 21-year-old was in Vietnam where he was killed in less than a month. Like everyone else in the community, I was staggered. The full evil of the war was now apparent; of what value was that which destroyed such a young man, which denied us his friendship, love, and compassion? No doubt an army chaplain offered the consolation that the fellow now was at peace in heaven. But how I doubted he had been put on earth to be destroyed, to be shot in the head on a battlefield while running to the aid of a fallen comrade. No, from the evil of war came only more evil. The cycle had to be broken. I made up my mind; I would refuse induction when the order came.

That spring of 1969, student riots closed many college campuses across the country. Black and minority student issues were frequently at the center, though white activist students, often from the Students for a Democratic Society, demanded an end to the university-based Reserve Officer Training Corps (ROTC), and an end to recruiting on campus by Dow Chemical Company, the manufacturer of napalm. Campuses that experienced rioting included: San Francisco State, San Mateo, San Fernando State, San Jose, Howard University, University of Massachusetts, Rice University, and Penn State.

Meanwhile in Vietnam, American combat deaths since the Paris peace talks began in May, 1968 reached 9,425. At

33,641, total combat deaths since January 1, 1961 passed the total for the Korean War. In response to increased Communist attacks, President Nixon said he was ruling out a cut in American forces in "the foreseeable future." In Fort Dix, New Jersey, a U.S. Army infantryman was found guilty of desertion and was sentenced to four years of hard labor and a dishonorable discharge. He had fled Vietnam for asylum in Sweden, the first soldier to be court-martialed for fleeing to a foreign country from Vietnam.

Upon learning of my intention to refuse induction, my friends at the Cafe urged me to see a draft counselor. Otherwise, they feared I was bound for prison. One friend knew of a lawyer-draft counselor in Pittsburgh who had been highly successful in helping young men with their draft problems; I saw no harm in talking to him.

A stocky, assertive man about 30, the counselor stated his approach at the outset: draft boards frequently made procedural errors, and often denied registrants the administrative remedies they were entitled to. When I explained the details of my case, especially the on-again/off-again I-A, he said clearly my local board had erred. If I followed his advice, he argued, we might well tie my case up for the next couple of years, by which time the war and draft would be over. Tie my case up? His parting words were, "why refuse induction and get into serious legal trouble if you don't have to?"

It was a persuasive argument; he was not talking about breaking laws, but rather of working within the system, using the same procedures as the Selective Service, but to my advantage not theirs. Still I had mixed emotions about it, mainly because it smacked of draft evasion; also, I was apprehensive because it meant squaring off with the draft board, with each aware the relationship would now be adversarial.

But what about draft evasion? Were it not for my friends at the Cafe I probably would not have considered it; I certainly would not have sought it out on my own. But I was vulnerable, anticipating an induction order any day, such that a quick solution was appealing; I was only human.

My friends argued that the bottom line was to deprive the military of young men to wage war with; *how* we deprived them was less important than the deprivation. I liked the notion.

As a result, I soon found myself in the evasion arena. Once again in Pittsburgh I stepped to the door of a private residence in the suburbs. When a small black boy answered the door, I told him Mac and I were from Morgantown, that we were there to see his father. Just then, the mother appeared and unlocked the screen door, my sensing such visits were occurring all the time now. She showed us into the modest living room where we sat and waited anxiously.

Presently, the doctor came in, the little boy tagging along to see exactly who these strangers were. Once seated, the child quickly lost interest and proceeded to make a nuisance of himself. With a quiet reprimand, the doctor sent him on his way; we smiled respectfully with his apology. The hour-and-a-half drive from Morgantown then dominated our conversation, although the doctor's weary face showed a fading patience.

"I like the music of Arthur Prysock," I suddenly blurted, the subject being the secret password.

The doctor's expression lifted. Acknowledging the password with a nod, he talked several minutes about Prysock, apparently genuinely his favorite artist.

"Which songs do you like?" he asked.

Mac and I looked at each other with blank faces. It was apparent these two white boys had no clue who Prysock was, though others might. Smiling, the doctor dropped the subject.

"Do you have anything in your medical history we might be able to build a letter around?" I was then asked, our now at the doctor's desk in the basement, the shelf above lined with organs in jars of formaldehyde illuminated by a bright florescent light.

"Well," I said with some embarrassment, "my heart tends to skip beats when I'm under stress," like at that moment, albeit prior medical exams had determined it was nothing serious.

Still it was sufficient, and with a few other general questions, he assured me the letter would be to me in a few days. I then thanked him with $50 in cash, his fee.

47

I knew nothing about this man, and as we left Pittsburgh I wondered if maybe I had not just been taken for $50. On the other hand, I had a sense about the "good doctor," as we called him; I believed him honorable. And while I disagreed with his charging a fee, I accepted the provision of this service as his way of protesting the war.

On April 26, 1969 I received the much anticipated and much dreaded Order to Report for Induction. I would now respond with either my heart or my head. Because I seemed stuck in that mode, I opted for the latter and phoned my counselor. His advice was simple enough; he said, "the board had already granted one postponement, though illegal; we should try it again." If they agreed to it, we could probably get a final postponement to finish the degree. So it was that I made the request, and to my astonishment was again granted a postponement, this time until the first call after August 19. That was all well and good, but now what was I going to do about the heart part, the part saying the war was evil and I should take a stand?

Was it my heart that caused me to turn in June when I overhead someone at the Cafe talking about one Reverend Hensley and the Universal Life Church in California? Again no. Because paying a nominal fee for ordainment sounded to me like a mere novelty, though as it turned out, a novelty used by some young men in the country for a IV-D ministerial deferment.

And so began my final "low road" choice, made as it was with the induction order now in my hand. Accordingly, Mac and I established the Morgantown chapter of the Universal Life Church.

Meanwhile, being ministers facilitated the peace activities we had already been organizing, inspired as we had been by an outing sponsored by the Episcopal campus ministry, called a "Celebration of Life". We held several of these through the summer, only to be upstaged in August by a much larger version of the same thing, called Woodstock.

# CHAPTER THREE
## THE COLD SWIM UPSTREAM

By midsummer 1969, President Nixon announced a new plan for the war; some 25,000 American troops were to be pulled out of Vietnam by August 31, part of what was termed "Vietnamization." Saigon troops would assume more of the burden of fighting. The move to cut the 540,000 man American force was hailed by GOP leaders in Congress, but some war critics scoffed at it as tokenism and a piecemeal withdrawal that would only lengthen the war. For me, it was a sign of hope. If the talk now was of de-escalation, could the end of the war be far off? This came as the American command disclosed that 5,656 of its aircraft, valued at $3 billion, had been lost in Vietnam since 1961.

On August 7, I received a response from the local board regarding my request for IV-D ministerial deferment. The letter did not contest the validity of the Universal Life Church, nor of my ordainment, but said that there was no evidence my ministerial activities were any more than an avocation; I would have to be ministering over 20 hours a week to be eligible for the IV-D. The rejection though was anticlimactic; as in the months since the application, I had settled on the broader category of conscientious objection, which was where I belonged all along, and no doubt where I would have been by now had I not gotten sidetracked.

At that, conscientious objection was intimidating. In recent months I had become familiar with the history of it, especially during World War II when there were some very inspiring cases, many involving imprisonment.

What I did not anticipate though, was how difficult it would be to translate my feelings into words that would make sense and convey sincerity to those wanting to draft me. Nonetheless, I formally submitted my application for conscientious objector status on August 15, 1969.

While I was trying to work within the system, some did not even register for the draft. One such young man was arrested by U.S. marshals outside the Cafe, while we stood unaware on the other side of the door. He was one of a growing number of individuals who considered the draft to be an invasion of privacy and a violation of basic human rights. For these persons, registering for the draft was an endorsement of war and involuntary servitude. It took great courage to hold this position, because one was likely to be arrested and probably jailed. Prosecution or immediate induction were usually the choices one was given when apprehended under these circumstances.

During World War II, total noncooperators embarrassed the government into creating and then expanding the classification of conscientious objection. It was just not fitting that the United States of America incarcerate citizens for their beliefs.

About a week before he was arrested, I had a brief conversation with the young man who was apprehended outside the Cafe. Younger than me, he was of slight build with frizzy brown-blond hair and a bushy mustache. Of the hippie circle, I guessed he was about 19 years old.

"Is it true you are not registered for the draft?" I asked. He knew I had registered and had just filed for conscientious objector classification.

"I can't relate to it at all," he said simply.

"So, do you intend to register eventually?" I asked. "I mean you could get into a lot of trouble if you don't, unless of course that's what you intend."

He replied, "I don't want to have anything to do with it, the draft, the war, not any of it. It's madness."

On the gut level, that was how I felt too. Still, while some might be able to avoid the draft by not registering, the odds were not good, as this young man found out.

A few days after the arrest, his girlfriend told us more about what happened: "He walked out of the Cafe around midnight, and there was an unmarked government car with two men inside, parked right at the front door." Her eyes were wide. "The moment they spotted him, they got out of the car and asked if he was so and so; not thinking, he said 'yes.' Of course, they would have found out anyway because they frisked him and checked his wallet. They then stuffed him into the back of the car and took him to jail."

As I stood there listening to her, I became furious. Her story sounded so much like tales of Nazi Germany, the gestapo at the door in the middle of the night. Yet this was happening in America. It was an outrage.

Later, when I learned this young man chose prison over induction, I applauded; he did not let the government intimidate him. But, I was still angry; what kind of choice was this, prosecution or immediate induction?

Afterwards, the Cafe was never the same; and if paranoia abounded, no one felt it more than me. For all I knew the next unmarked car out front waited for me.

Filing for conscientious objector status involved writing a detailed explanation of one's views by completing Selective Service Form 150. In the first section, I had to sign one of two statements indicating whether I was claiming noncombatant status, classification I-A-O, or alternative civilian service, I-O. I chose the latter.

In the next section, I was required to explain the basic beliefs by which I lived, why I thought they were religious and how they led me to conscientious objection. By this time the Supreme Court had broadened the definition of religious beliefs; that is, CO applicants no longer had to base a claim on membership in a church or even hold a conventional belief in God. Then, in *U.S. v. Seeger*, the court went even further. They made it clear that a man could qualify for recognition as a CO if he had a belief in his life that paralleled the more traditional religious beliefs of others who obviously qualified for CO status. As a result of this ruling, those who lived by some "guiding principle" that prevented them from participating in war could qualify for conscientious objector status.

I REFUSE

The second question asked how one's beliefs developed. In response, I provided a chronological description of religious training, education and life experience. Were I only 18 years old, my answer might have been brief. But because I was older, and had already received an induction notice, I was able to give a very complete history demonstrating how my beliefs matured.

The next question asked CO applicants to explain why they were unable to serve in the Medical Corps. Again I-A-Os usually trained to serve as medics. Here I explained how I could not in good conscience participate in any organization, in any capacity, whose primary purpose was to wage war.

The final question of this series was meant to measure one's sincerity. I was asked how I tried to live according to my beliefs, as evidenced by entering social service, religious work, antiwar or civil rights activity.

In the final section, one provided further evidence of sincerity by including articles or school papers one might have written, newspaper clippings, speeches, and supportive letters from family, friends, clergy, teachers or others. I provided nine letters of support.

At first glance Form 150 looked simple enough, but it was extremely difficult to answer. How did you present this information in a convincing manner, knowing that those who read it most certainly had a different view and were apt to be unhappy that you disagreed with it?

An adequate response to these questions could not be jotted down in an hour; I spent days laboring over the essays that became my answers. Still, I worried that my edits left the final version sounding clinical and lifeless. My biggest problem came from being raised in a family, a community, a country which taught males not to express their feelings and emotions. My father, for example, was extremely controlled this way; my brother and I followed his example. "We are not a demonstrative family," my mother was wont to say.

Even other people in the neighborhood, middle-class families like ours and blue-collar families, were much the same. I suspected it was the result of World War II, living in a militarized society which held high the soldier who was bold, courageous, and controlled; a similar image was also projected in American Western movies.

Still, our culture was not unlike that of many countries where it was considered a sign of weakness for a man to show certain emotions, especially those suggesting vulnerability. But was not vulnerability what spirituality was?

I suspected the draft board was not likely to see it that way, so in defense I tried to be macho to be sure I would be believed; if not macho, very analytical, the style of men.

At one point I threw my pen down, deeming these questions about myself and my beliefs as really none of their business. Besides, was it not all insanity? At age 18, young men were required to register for induction into an organization which trained them to kill, and if they refused, they would be arrested and put in jail. This was not to say that once registered, once in the machine, one could not request deferment or exemption. But it had to be on the government's terms, especially if you were a conscientious objector.

Completing Form 150 was an enormously frustrating and anger provoking experience. But what could I do? It had to be filled out. One either completed the form or had nothing to do with any of it and became a noncooperator.

Still, one part of this process was a great morale booster; the people I asked for letters of support were ready and generous, as embarrassing as it was to approach friends, neighbors, and employers to write on my behalf. All in all though, as I put the letters together in an envelope with the completed Form 150, I could not help but feel my claim would be successful.

As it happened, it was all for naught; the local board wasted no time issuing a new induction order, this time for September 8th. If I was furious at filling out Form 150, I was doubly so now, because I was at a loss as to what was next—if in fact there was anything left but to refuse and go to jail. All I could do was phone the draft counselor in Pittsburgh, though I suspected he would be unhappy with me for not sticking to his postponement strategy; he knew nothing about my filing for conscientious objector status. As it turned out, that I felt compelled to file apparently spoke for itself.

"Your filing for conscientious objector classification represented a change in your point of view, which should have automatically reopened your file for full reevaluation," he said. "Obviously, all they want to do now is induct you. But by denying you a full reevaluation, they have erred legally. They have denied you your rights, and I think they know it."

"I'm supposed to report for induction in two weeks," I said. "I put everything I felt into that CO application. They ignored it. My feeling now is to hell with them. They can take their induction order and shove it. I'll just refuse."

"When you refuse induction, everything changes," he warned. "It's then a matter for the courts to decide, and that's not to your advantage. The longer we can keep this with the Selective Service, the better your chances for an appropriate classification."

He told me the next step was to request a "personal appearance," as it was called, where I could argue my case in front of the board. Five days later, I sat in a sterile little room, institutional beige in color. A quorum of three of the five board members were there pondering my claim. We sat at a short, rectangular metal table, at which the board made their monthly judgements.

It appeared I was the only one there on business. I wore a shirt and tie, and they were dressed in sport clothes like they had just come from watching a ball game. Then there were their smiles, as though they were entertained by the novelty of me. When was the last time they had a CO application, a I-O no less? They did have a I-A-O once in a while. Too bad about those two local boys, those medics killed in Vietnam. Heroes. And now here is this young fellow wanting civilian alternative service. . . .

Their dislike of me was all over their faces. Still, there we sat as I restated the basis for my opposition to the war and to military service, all of which they had in writing in front of them.

Was it because some of them were military veterans that they had a deaf ear for what I was saying? It was not that they were hostile toward me, but they did not seem interested or have a clue about what I was saying. Originally, I thought it was just me, being nervous, perhaps I did not explain myself well.

"My conscientious objection has evolved over many years," I again explained. "That evolution peaked with the first induction order you sent me this year. As you know, the law identifies what is called 'late developing conscientious objection,' meaning the objection does not crystalize until late. In such cases, one suspects he is opposed to armies and wars, but cannot know how real that opposition is until he is presented an actual order to report to an army or to war." They did not know what I was talking about. In light of that, I thought there might be more participation on their part, a question and answer period which would have benefitted us both. Instead, the 71-year-old member told me war stories, the others asking what my parents thought of what I was doing. They treated me as though I were an errant little boy. Shame on me for doing something that my parents would scold me for. Obviously, they had overlooked or forgotten the letter from my father stating his full support of my claim.

The old man's stories about his regiment in Europe might have been interesting and entertaining were it not obvious that his intent was to inspire me. I guess he thought I would suddenly see the light and report for induction that very afternoon. But if his goal was to inspire, all he did was anger me by talking like I was some dim-witted bumpkin, and the implication by the others that I was merely misguided was insulting.

Of course, on the assumption there was going to be more substance to the meeting, I had prepared for questions such as: are you against all wars, or only the war in Vietnam? What method would you use to resist evil? Why is it wrong to defend your country's interests? Why did you register in accordance with a law passed to raise an army? Do you object to others being drafted, or only yourself? What about the Christian doctrine of approval of "just wars?" But no such questions came and the meeting ended, a complete waste of time.

That night at the Cafe I ranted and raved in frustration. Had they asked, I would have told them I was against all wars, with the understanding that the Vietnam War was the one in question, the one directly affecting me. What I would have done during World War II, or what I would do in some future war, I could not know. I knew the opposition I hoped I would feel and would express, but it could only be speculation.

As for evil invading my household, it was unrealistic to think I would stand idly by while a lunatic slaughtered my family. Situational ethics, and "selective pacifism" were applicable here, whereby one reserved the right to protect one's life. This was a different issue from conscientious objection which focused only on opposition to war.

This is not to say the issues of selective pacifism and opposition to war are unrelated. A favorite example is the pacifistic Taoist who, on discovering an intruder in his house, uses force only as a "regrettable necessity." Even then, he goes only as far as is needed to stop the offense. This attitude extended to the general who despite being victorious on the battlefield, was received home with rites of mourning.[20]

At the heart of this was the belief in the sanctity of human life, indeed of all life. Because I shared this view, how could I not react with horror to scenes of B-52 bombers with their 19 tons of munitions per plane, systematically destroying everything in their path—men, women, children, plants, animals, insects, everything?

Soon after, I studied the Selective Service rules and regulations to understand why my meeting with the board had gone as it had. My counselor was correct in stating that any change in my way of thinking should have resulted in a "reopening" of my classification, or file. But the fact that an induction order had already been issued meant the board was under no obligation to reopen.

This was not to say they would not listen to me; they did, sort of. However, it was not considered an official "personal appearance." Rather was it an "interview," as the regulations called it, also known as a "courtesy hearing," which did not require the board to do any more than sit there. The State Director of the Selective Service, I then learned, was my only recourse; he had the power to cancel or postpone inductions, order files to be reopened, or advance cases to the State Appeal Board.

In the meantime, "Vietnamization" had the first 25,000 of the 540,000 American troops out of the war, but it had no immediate effect at home, as men were still being drafted. My induction date was still set for September 8, 1969. Accordingly, I wrote a letter of appeal to the State Director.

20. Holmes Welch, *Taoism: The Parting of the Way* (Boston: Beacon Press, 1957), p. 25; Wing Tsit-Chan, *The Way of Lao Tzu* (New York: Bobbs-Merrill, 1963), p. 154.

It seemed to me the State Board was the answer, consisting as it did of five individuals nominated by the governor and appointed by the President. Members included, "one member from labor, one from industry, one physician, one lawyer, and where applicable, one member from agriculture."

As September 8th approached, then passed, my confidence grew. I believed the State Director had determined the worthiness of my claim, and had ordered the matter to the State Board. I had no reason to doubt that they would vote in my favor and approve the I-O classification.

I always assumed that a I-O was harder to get than a I-A-O, because those with I-O classification did not serve in the armed forces; their induction into civilian service could not be used to fill draft quotas. Nevertheless, at the time, there seemed to be more I-Os being granted, another reason for optimism.

Those granted the I-O classification gave their local boards a list of up to three types of work which they would be willing and able to perform. However, many boards insisted that a I-O choose a civilian work assignment from lists they provided. These lists included organizations which often employed COs and had general approval from the state and national director of the Selective Service.

I speculated that since most of the jobs on the local board lists were in general hospitals, mental institutions, and old age or children's homes, I would request a job better suited to my interests and abilities. For example, some boards had approved work in medical research, forestry, settlement houses, agricultural research, state highway and sanitation departments, United Nations agencies, poverty programs, education, legal aid, and draft counseling. While the Peace Corps could not be approved, similar programs were, including overseas work sponsored by private and religious organizations.

I imagined myself serving in Volunteers in Service to America (VISTA). This was a government organization, not unlike the Peace Corps, which sent volunteers to help people and communities in poverty-stricken, rural areas like Appalachia, including West Virginia.

Some men who qualified as conscientious objectors, but were opposed to both military service and alternative civilian service, even rejected I-O status; for them it was still involuntary servitude. Working with VISTA would be a contradiction for them, because they would be working for a volunteer organization under the penalty of law.

As it happened, this was not to be my problem. I should have been suspicious when a reply came from the State Director in three weeks; appeals normally took up to three months. Opening the letter, I read that the Director had denied me access to the higher board; he turned the matter back to the local board for review. Accordingly, a new induction order was issued for October 6th.

While shaken, I understood why this happened. Late claims of conscientious objection were the most difficult to get recognized and were often viewed with suspicion. To understand this was to understand the definition of conscientious objection as outlined in the Military Selective Service Act of 1967:

Nothing contained in this title shall be construed to require any person to be subject to combatant training and service in the armed forces of the United States who, by reason of religious training and belief, is conscientiously opposed to participation to war in any form. As used in this subsection, the term 'religious training and belief' does not include essentially political, sociological, or philosophical views, or merely a personal moral code.

The assumption was that one's religious training and belief would have him balking when he registered at age 18; he would identify himself as a CO on the registration form. On the other hand, should his viewpoint mature or crystalize after the receipt of an induction order, as precedented by U.S. v. Gearey,[21] one could declare later, like I did. In such instances, however, considerable explanation was required, explanation demonstrating that the late claim represented "a change in the registrant's status resulting from circumstances over which he had no control."

It was an ironic requirement in my case, because the circumstances over which I had no control, and which prompted my CO claim was their induction order. The only way they

21. U.S. v. Gearey, 368 F.2d 144 (1966).

could measure the credibility of my claim then was by my sincerity, but how could that be done?

The law, reflecting how hard it was to explain religious convictions, much less to prove one held them, said the board could not turn down an individual's claim merely because it was doubtful or felt one had not "proved" it. Indeed, in *Dickinson v. U.S.*,[22] the courts ruled a CO claim could not arbitrarily be turned down by a skeptical draft board. Only on the basis of facts in the individual's file indicating that a claim might be insincere, would a federal court uphold the rejection of a CO claim. However, all this was academic for me, as October 6, 1969 was now my induction date.

Because of construction on the interstate highway, I decided the state road to the west would be the better bet, though it would mean a six-hour round trip. So it was that the two lane road led me along the Ohio River to Parkersburg, before dropping straight south to Charleston. Unusually cold and gray for late September, it misted rain enough to make a grimy mess of the windshield, dead leaves catching in the wiper blades.

I had not made an appointment with the State Director thinking I might be turned back. My plan was to confront him and make a personal plea; that is, to cancel the induction order and permit my appeal to the State Board. But my frustration would only continue, for upon arrival at the Selective Service State Headquarters, I learned the general was not in. Indeed, he would not be available all that week; I could, however, make an appointment. If the drive seemed long and miserable on the way there, it felt doubly so on the way back.

For the next seven days, I expected a phone call from the Director's office canceling the appointment on the grounds there was nothing more to discuss. When no call came though, suddenly I was hopeful again. I knew the odds were not good, but as I was to be inducted in less than two weeks, I had to keep trying.

When at last the day came for my appointment, I was in much better humor. Once more I wound my way down the narrow road flanking the Ohio River, and then through the tree-thick hills of Jackson County, to Charleston. The sun was

22. *Dickinson v. U.S.*, 346 U.S. 389 (1953).

out, the remaining autumn leaves flickering their colors in the crisp air. Nor was finding the office a problem as before; in fact, I was 30 minutes early. It gave me time to review what I wanted to say to the Director.

When finally the hour of the appointment came, I took a deep breath and tried to relax, reminding myself I would probably be in there at least 30 minutes. Closing my tie, I got out of the car and strode into the building.

"Come," came a deep voice at the end of the long, dark office; why he wanted it so dark when it was a bright sunny day, I did not know. As such, the venetian blinds were all but shut, the shadows at the bookcases and heavy furniture along the long walls made the room look quite Gothic. I spotted the general seated down at the end. And he remained seated, hunched over a stack of papers illuminated by a single narrow desk lamp. Not looking up, he told me to sit down in a chair in the shadows to his right; moments of silence then passed until finally his hard eyes raised.

"What can I do for *you*?" he asked, obviously not knowing who I was.

"My name is Donald Simons," I replied confidently. "I filed for conscientious objector classification in Morgantown, though you may not recall the case. I identified it with your aide when I made this appointment last week. I'm here to again ask for appeal to the State Board."

The Director was not paying attention, his eyes having returned to the papers on his desk.

"Otherwise," I continued, "can you tell me what I am to do now, what recourse I have?"

Several moments passed, until he again looked up; he was clearly annoyed. "My advice to you, young man," he droned, "is to submit to induction. Good day."

I had been there less than five minutes, whereupon I dragged again to the car for the long drive back home.

What a feeling of desperation! I had so built up this man and the possibilities of him rendering justice in my case, that to abruptly and unequivocally have those hopes dashed once and for all, made me feel like jumping off a bridge. All I could think of on the drive back was, now what? Without help from the State Director, how could I continue my fight? Was I not out of legal options? This was to say nothing of the time factor; with induction day less than a week away, there could be no further written correspondence on the matter.

In the absence of legal options, I had only illegal ones, which of course was to the government's advantage; with this added pressure, surely they assumed I would submit. Obviously, what they did not anticipate was my renewed resolve to resist.

I did not show up for the October 6th induction date. It caused my counselor some alarm when I phoned to say I had exhausted my administrative remedies as he advised and had gone as far as the State Director would allow. My fate was now sealed, he confided, meaning an indictment would be next. It was what he had hoped we could avoid, because now there would be a whole new set of problems.

The thought of an indictment was frightening. For the first time I felt like I was in over my head.

# CHAPTER FOUR

## I REFUSE

The beginning of the second phase of "Vietnamization," and the withdrawal of another 60,000 troops from the war, did not alter plans for the October 15, 1969 Moratorium Day, a peace event unprecedented in American history. Thousands across the country participated in rallies, marches, and church services. Meanwhile, those supporting the war urged people to drive with their headlights on and to fly the flag at full-mast, in opposition to the Moratorium's half-staff.

At West Virginia University, there were a range of Moratorium activities, including lectures at a "Freedom School," an antiwar teach-in, a fast, a vigil, and a rally on the Memorial Plaza. There was a showing of the film by Emile de Antonio, *In the Year of the Pig*, that featured historic Western and Communist newsreel to argue the folly of French and American involvement in Vietnam.

There was also a memorial service on the Courthouse Square, that included the placing of a wreath in honor of the war dead, a concert for peace, and a candlelight service. The conservative voice was represented by the Interfraternity Council, which condemned the Moratorium and its sponsors.

Wearing a black arm band, like many of the participants, Mac and I attended the memorial service at Saint John's Chapel on campus. The service began with everyone singing the antiwar song "Blowin' in the Wind," made popular by the folk group Peter, Paul and Mary, and continued with a prayer by the Presbyterian chaplain. Words commemorating the war dead were offered by the Methodist chaplain, followed by poetry and a folk song from a Vietnam veteran, another prayer by the Catholic chaplain, and the singing of the mournful folk song "Kum-baya."

A silent procession followed the service, participants winding their way the several blocks to the Courthouse Square. Damp and dreary, the day invited a huddling close; at the square, the people packed three sides of the elevated stage erected for the event. As speaker after speaker addressed the somber crowd from a public address system, I watched and listened from the center, 10 feet from the stage.

Past my eyes and rising overhead was the courthouse clock tower, a structure I seemingly had been born with, having walked by it a thousand times on the way to school or to shop on High Street. To the left was a short avenue called Chancery Row, home of the town's law establishment; adjacent to it the offices of the county sheriff and the county jail, all in grayed red brick like the courthouse itself.

To the right was Walnut Street, a short walk to the Cafe. But the Cafe regulars were not well-represented on the square. Most of them were on campus for the other events. Before the day was out, Mac and I would be there too, to hear some of the more political speeches at the rally on Memorial Plaza.

It was quite a different feeling at the Plaza. For example, one young man interrupted his statement to the largely student crowd with a finger pointed toward the back row. "Lest we forget, 'Big Brother' is watching," he shouted, referring to the omnipresent government in George Orwell's novel *1984*. As everyone turned, sure enough there was a man conspicuously filming everyone present. The man immediately stuffed the camera into his jacket, but not before someone grabbed for it. As the crowd started booing him, he quickly scooped up his gear and scampered off. Whether he was actually a government agent or not, no one knew, but at that moment we all believed it. The government was not only at war with the Vietnamese, but again, it was up against its own people.

I did not attend the "Freedom School," or *In the Year of the Pig*, simply because I was not politically motivated in my opposition to the war. I participated in events that, I thought, would best show my respect for those serving and dying in Vietnam, even though I disagreed with their going, and believed that what they were being made to do was criminal. I was most struck and moved by the strong turnout among the townspeople, suggesting some in our largely conservative community were having a change of heart. Mostly, however, I appreciated that the day put my CO efforts back into their larger context. That is, the evil of the war was the real issue, including what it was doing to the country, pitting sons against fathers, husbands against wives and neighbors against neighbors.

Although my spirits were lifted by the Moratorium, two days later they came crashing down again; I received yet another induction order, the third in as many months, the fourth of the year. I wondered if this was some kind of joke. Did the Selective Service think I was frightened and would welcome the opportunity to submit?

The draft board office was located on the third floor of a faded, yellow brick building with metal windows and venetian blinds. Armed Forces recruiters shared the floor, their crackerbox offices vying for visitors' attention as one walked the narrow hallway to the last door on the right.

I had dealt face-to-face with the draft board clerk on several occasions, a bland woman who replaced an old lady whose retirement had long been overdue. Though they had no real legal authority, these clerks wielded considerable influence; actually, they made most of the day-to-day decisions. The results were then approved by the board members, who often met only once a month.

I would say this clerk and I were friends inasmuch as she had expressed concern for me a time or two. Violating draft law led to a great deal of legal trouble, and even prison, she reminded me, not without her bias.

"I don't know what you people are trying to do," I declared walking in the door. "What's this new induction order for November 3rd? Why do you keep sending me induction orders when you know my position?"

She put on her best cool, defensive face.

"It's regulations, Mr. Simons. For all we know, you want to challenge the draft law in court. There are established procedures for that, and we have to get our part right. As for your failing to appear for induction on October 6th, you didn't tell us what happened. We have had inductees oversleep, you know."

"Oversleep?"

Her face softened.

"We also have young men who, like you, have filed for CO status, and not succeeding, have changed their minds."

"My mind is made up."

"But you've got to be present on the induction date," she said standing. "You can refuse at the appropriate time in the proceedings, but you must go through the initial phase. That's why we gave you a new induction date."

I did not believe her. I sensed the plan was to get me there, then to either intimidate me into complying, or to induct me before I knew what happened.

"If you intend a court challenge," she continued, "then sooner or later you will have to be present at an induction date. Litigation cannot begin until the Selective Service part of it is concluded."

This was totally absurd; I could not believe it. I was telling them they could take their induction order and stick it, and they were saying okay, but it had to be done according to rules and regulations.

On the other hand, I noted how she kept mentioning court and litigation, no doubt suspecting I was nervous about the prospect. And she was right. She was more than right; I could hear the confidence in her voice. She knew from experience that the chances were slim for a draft case succeeding in court if it was not resolved by the Selective Service System; in theory, a registrant was given every opportunity to make his case without having to resort to the courts. In reality though, it did not necessarily work that way, and I was living proof.

I had nothing else to say to the clerk beyond shaking my head, and storming back down the hall. Why did I get the impression she was enjoying this? Her eyes said, "Simons, the poor little college student. He should grow up, be more like a man, like the guys from the mines and the farms; they didn't make such a fuss."

# I REFUSE

Frank is the name I will give the young man previously described as having a support group of student activists who helped him in his confrontation with the system. A teacher in the local schools, his initial contact with the activists was to try to coordinate activities between university students and miners struggling for black lung benefits. Black lung was a respiratory illness brought on by years of breathing coal dust. Frank's father-in-law was a miner and a union activist, so Frank was no stranger to nonviolent resistance. Before his personal struggle was all over, however, Frank found himself consumed by the cult of violence and revolution; suddenly Mao was his hero, not Gandhi.

Over the years Frank and I crossed paths three times. We had competed against each other in a school-wide sporting event in junior high school, had studied martial arts together, and had attended the same "World Religions" class, ironically the religions of the Far East including Vietnam.

In short, I knew Frank to be an emotional man, a man of great passion toward things he believed. If there was a problem, it was that his emotionality made him susceptible to losing perspective, hence to being swept away by the tides of the times.

I had a mixture of feelings on encountering fellow-draftee Frank at the November 3rd induction "send-off" ceremony, an event sponsored by the local Veterans of Foreign Wars. This ceremony was a long-standing tradition in many communities, being the last time family and friends would see a draftee until his return from basic training.

For some reason, there were no parents present on this day. However, Frank was there accompanied by six activist friends grouped around him. It was obvious they were not there to see him go into the army. Our thorough and efficient local board clerk was also there checking off the names of the draftees as we arrived.

"Good morning," I said leaning toward her. "I'm not staying. I just wanted you to see for the record that I did show up for an induction date."

She looked pleased, but anxious to correct me. "Oh, but you can't go just yet. You must stay long enough to get instructions."

"Instructions?" I said. "For what? I'm not being inducted."
"Please have a seat, Mr. Simons. You'll understand more in
a few minutes." With suddenly mounting anxiety, I sat by
myself at a table near the front door.

The room reminded me of a cafeteria, with heavy metal,
pedestaled tables and lightly cushioned, armless metal chairs.
The gray formica table tops were sticky from the complimen-
tary coffee, a beverage not consumed by Frank's delegation or
by me; drowsiness was not our problem. Besides, we did not
want to be made to feel welcome.

The clerk and the director of the local Red Cross moved to
the front tables to give instructions and to offer inspiration. To
their left, a large American flag stood militarily, as three
other inductees, in the first row, looked on with anticipation.
Just then there was a camera flash; I looked over to see the
local newspaper photographer aiming at Frank's group, their
fists raised defiantly.

The "instructions" the clerk referred to was her first order
of business; she advised everyone how to get to the induction
center in the neighboring town, should anyone wish to go by
car rather than in the bus provided. To my dismay I found out
that I would have to go to the induction center to formally
register my refusal to be inducted. With no further need for
me to be there I left, shuddering in disgust as the director of
the local Red Cross began cooing his inspirational remarks.

For most people this process began harmlessly enough, or so
it seemed, with the words on the induction notice, "You are
hereby ordered to report . . ." But this was only the beginning
of the ordering. Once in the army it would be all orders, commands one was bound to obey, right to the order to kill, which
one's survival instincts would have him do, and do many times
over regardless of the psychological and spiritual consequences.

"Thou shalt not kill," our religions taught, though our gov-
ernments contend thou shalt kill under certain political circumstances. One had better follow the government's line or
there was the threat of prosecution and prison. For most, that
threat canceled the moral choice.

For instance, a friend asked with concern if I was aware that
refusing induction was a federal offense, and that I could be

imprisoned, as if that was what was important, not the nation's blindness to the moral catastrophe which was the continuing war.

Perhaps this friend's myopia helped to keep him from feeling the guilt this war generated in all of us. Some, like veterans of previous wars, found their way around it by an excess of patriotism, by embracing the government which had also given them the license to kill. The hawk veterans organizations were a case in point, members of the "my country, love it or leave it" crowd. Of course, should one leave, he would not be welcomed back; because those that did leave symbolized the nation's moral failing, something that even the hawks felt beneath their flags, ribbons, and medals. To get around this, some hawks went on to become members of local draft boards, believing wrongly that by ushering others to war they would not feel so bad.

The saddest consequence of this was the perpetuation of an attitude where the military and war were seen as something good. Accordingly, draftees were treated to these send-off ceremonies with a hardy handshake, a pat on the back, and assurances they were doing the right thing for God and country. In fact it was the wrong thing; the truth is, humans killing humans is a moral offense of the highest magnitude, and no government has the right to order it.

Obviously, Frank and his group felt the same way, they stayed to interrupt and heckle the Red Cross director for the remainder of his speech.

The people sitting with Frank could often be seen handing out radical literature at folding tables around campus. Members of a local organization called the Student Activist League (SAL), they believed in what was termed, "the politics of confrontation." Many of the members of this ad hoc group also worked in the "Mountaineer Freedom Party," (MFP) a liberal front party involved in university student elections. In an October 1, 1969 article in the conservative *Morgantown Post*, the SAL was listed among the radical groups most likely to perpetuate violence at West Virginia University.

Other groups identified as potential "troublemakers" were the American Civil Liberties Union (ACLU) and the Young Americans for Freedom (YAF). The SAL, MFP, and ACLU were designated as "left wing," but the YAF was a right-wing organization whose local chapter was quoted as prepared "to crush the hippies and their communistic takeover." Soon after their national founding in 1960, the YAF claimed a membership of 30,000 students and young adults, with representation on 200 campuses. Like their left-wing counterparts, the YAF devoted much attention to the Vietnam War; their mass meetings, petitions, and blood donor campaigns were mounted to show support for the war.

By such means they hoped to apply pressure on the Administration for a "harder" line in Vietnam. They favored increased bombing of North Vietnam and other forms of escalation of the war to insure an American "victory."

Among the left-wing groups the MFP was the least radical, promoting civil rights for blacks, and the abolition of grades; the SAL, however, wanted to radicalize the campus; the ACLU, "the most clandestine" of the organizations, sought civil liberties issues to take to court.

Conspicuously absent from the list was the Students for a Democratic Society (SDS), a group active on campus for two years prior to June 1969; by that fall, however, it seemed to be replaced by the SAL. That the founder of the local SDS was graduating, might have been the reason, along with SDS becoming too radical to be successful on a conservative West Virginia campus.

As it was, in the 1960s, the SDS was the largest, best known, and most influential student political group in the country. In the book *SDS*, author Kirkpatrick Sale traces the roots of the organization to 1905. Once called the League for Industrial Democracy, and then the Student League for Industrial Democracy, it was not until its reorganization (1960–1962), that it truly blossomed as a political force. From 1962 to 1965, SDS aggressively challenged American institutions to live up to American ideals. By 1968 chapters extended coast to coast; and by 1969, the goal of the now completely radical SDS was the thorough, and for some violent, overthrow of the American system.

I knew the local SDS leader through a jointly attended World Religions course. A class of few students, which included Frank, we were all smiles when this much publicized campus figure walked in the door; it would be fun having a

70

political celebrity in our midst. Short, with wavy auburn hair, wide eyes and a toothy grin, this young man did not look like the head of an activist political group. He moved into that arena at the end of his freshman year in college partly because of an essay he wrote defending the Vietnam War. "Before I left the room," he said, "I realized all the reasons I'd written were absurd."

The next year, he spent time at the local Methodist church where he had lengthy discussions with the pastor about how to respond to the war. The pastor subsequently risked the ire of his congregation by letting the young man hold political meetings there.

"I've always had a love-hate affair with the church," said the SDS leader. "I thought I should be a minister, but I'm not religious enough." In his view, the church played the role of an apologist for society, or a first aid rescuer for the downtrodden. "I am neither," he said. "I'd just like to be left alone, but the world won't let that happen. What it does to me, and to other people bothers me. . . ."

His words were matched by action. In the summer of 1966 he joined the Freedom Riders on a bus to Memphis, Tennessee where he marched with nationally known civil rights leaders. He also organized the Student Action for Appalachian Progress, which tutored students in the hollows of the local county, and worked with student-miner groups in support of black lung legislation.

Such work was not always appreciated by the more conservative factions on campus. Two incidents in 1967 were characteristic of what he and the SDS endured. On one occasion he attempted to speak against the war in the courtyard of a residence hall. Surrounded closely by the multi-story buildings, the courtyard was a natural setting for a speech of any kind; it was clever of him to choose it. Still, it did not take long for the conservative faction in the residences to express a counter opinion: he was bombarded by buckets of water from windows, and the sound of a record player blaring "Stars and Stripes Forever."

Another confrontation occurred just before exams in the spring of 1967, on the occasion of what the SDS titled, "Gentle Thursday." It was supposed to be an afternoon of singing, sitting on lawns, throwing frisbees, carrying balloons, and drawing on the sidewalks with colored chalk, all as a statement for freedom of expression.

Because it rained on Thursday, the event was moved to Friday, some 20 long-haired SDS members and friends gathered on the lawn outside a lecture hall. Sitting in a circle, around a bamboo pole sporting balloons, the participants sang to a guitar, burned incense, and handed out flowers and candy.

But it was Friday, and soon the gathering was surrounded by a hundred beer-fueled fraternity members, identifiable by their blue vinyl jackets emblazoned with Greek letters. Quickly, the mood grew ugly, some eyewitnesses saying it felt like a lynching was about to occur. All the while, campus security police stood by, but did nothing to keep the large circle of Greeks from closing in on the SDS.

Returning to the event after attending a meeting, the SDS leader was shocked to see what was happening. "Don't go any closer," he was warned by two leaders of the right-wing Young Americans for Freedom, who stood by as a shield hoping to deflect the impression that their organization condoned the bullying of liberals.

Words were then exchanged, prompting the Greeks to rush in, destroy all the balloons, and drag the SDSers away. One activist, a young girl, tried to cling to the bamboo pole only to be shaken loose. Several of the participants were forced to crawl through a line of Greeks who ridiculed them and threatened them with burning cigarettes. The campus police still made no attempt to intervene. Just then, a group of black football and basketball players formed a human wedge, broke through the ranks of the Greeks, and led the shaken SDSers to safety.[23]

"I had visions of the Alabama police clubbing people who were sitting down not harming anybody," said the basketball player who spearheaded the wedge. Ironically, he was an ex-Marine. One was left to wonder whether it was this kind of humiliation which led to the formation of the more rhetorically violent SAL.

23. Bonni McKeown, *Peaceful Patriot: The Story of Tom Bennett* (Charleston, West Virginia: Mountain State Press, 1980), p. 144.

I respected the SDS leader even though I never really knew what to say to him. His politics and methods were not mine, albeit as time went on, it was surprising how close I got.

The induction center in the neighboring town was not the one I was previously sent to for my pre-induction physical exam. Checking the address, I drove through the neighborhood twice before finally spotting it. As my heart pounded anxiously, I pulled into the parking lot and tried to calm myself; after all, I was probably only there for a simple matter, like signing a form to refuse induction.

Out of the car, I marched through the two sets of glass doors, across the narrow lobby, and to an enlisted man at the front desk.

"May I help you?" he asked.

"I'm from Morgantown, and was supposed to be inducted today, but I want to refuse. Can you tell me how to go about doing that?"

He stared at me a moment, stunned; he looked down, then back up again. "I'll be right back. Have a seat."

I crossed the room to a row of well-worn chairs, but because I was nervous, chose not to sit. Instead I went back to the glass doors, where I saw it was beginning to snow.

Returning, the enlisted man informed me that before I could refuse, I would have to take the induction physical exam.

"You must be kidding," I said.

"Those are regulations."

Suddenly the whole picture flashed before me: the local board clerk said I had to be present on the induction date; then I was told I had to go to the induction center; now I had to take the physical exam. It was a set-up after all. They planned to induct me.

"Those men over there are going in for the physical in a few minutes," said the enlisted man. "You can go with them."

I said nothing, returning to the glass doors to rethink the situation. There was nothing to keep me from walking out again, I reminded myself, though I also wondered if I was not making more of this than there really was; perhaps I was just being paranoid. The Selective Service and the military could not trick someone, could not induct a guy without his knowing it. That would be illegal. On the other hand, had they not gotten me this far? After all, here I was standing in the induction center.

Just inside the physical examination room was a changing area, but with no lockers or benches. There was, however, an L-shaped shelf across the end wall and down one side, where clothes could be stashed in individual mounds. Stripped to my shorts, it was a matter of going from station to station, assembly line style, being weighed, having eyes checked, ears inspected, and so on down the anatomy. I was fortunate to be in a small group this time, unlike the previous physical which was truly a cattle drive.

Expediency, I supposed, was the principal reason for the group approach, though the psychological effect was surely part of it. The purpose was to undermine individuality. An army needed homogeneity more than individuality. Which was not to say the medical staff was overbearing; they were good-natured and went about their routine as though it was merely a job. Indeed, some of the inductees looked admiringly on these staffers, impressed by their emblems and stripes. That too was part of the psychology, I was sure. I saw this before, in high school, when the local recruiters came to dazzle the guys. It was pure deception, then and now, an attempt to mask what a soldier really was, what an army really did. Sadly, those impressed young men who were with me in that induction center assembly line would discover the truth soon enough.

With the completion of the physical exam, I was directed to an office down the hall, the office of the head medical officer. Inside, I sat uncomfortably on a metal chair by the door, my bare feet fidgeting on the spotless, cold tile floor. Presently then, in strode a tall, hefty Marine Corps captain-physician; he greeted me with a thick Southern accent.

"I've read this letter from your doctor," he said, flashing the page in his hand. "Tell me, how do you feel right now?"

"Not too bad," I said uncertainly, if not caught by surprise.

"Can you describe your symptoms for this problem of yours," he asked as he plopped down and leaned back in his big chair.

That I was being asked for the symptoms struck me as quite

funny, though I dared not crack a smile. The doctor in Pittsburgh had urged me to study the symptoms he had outlined, so if asked I would sound convincing. I failed to review them, an indication of my lack of commitment to this approach.

"Well," I said, trying my best, "my heart skips beats under stress. . . ."

Hooking on his stethoscope, the officer rose and began checking here and there around my heart. After several minutes, he returned to his desk, pondered briefly, only to pick up the telephone. Dialing, he again tilted back in his chair, as I looked on in bewilderment.

When the person on the other end answered, the captain stated cordially that he had a young man there at the Armed Forces Induction Center, who had a letter from that office. I closed my eyes. But when I opened them again, I discovered the officer still talking to the "good doctor," who said he recalled my case, that he had observed thus and so, and that in his opinion I was not fit for military service. A smile of appreciation came to my face; he could just as easily have denied knowing me. Following some technical talk, the captain hung up.

But alas, it was for naught. Rather, it was now one for, and one against disqualification. A third opinion was needed, and for that I would have to go over to the local hospital, though I preferred to forget about the whole thing.

"It's late afternoon," said the officer, his Southern drawl rising. "You can make the hospital today, but you'll have to come back here tomorrow to finish your processing."

Nodding, I thanked him, I was not sure why, and departed. Mostly though, I was annoyed because I knew what the third opinion would be, and were it not for my playing this game, I probably would have had the refusal of induction papers signed by then.

But, it appeared fate had other things in mind for me, who knew the dynamics of it? Quite possibly there was some unfinished spiritual business being worked out here, business requiring more than a doctor's letter.

It was a bright, sunny, cold morning as I again drove the 20 miles to the induction center, with the knowledge this day was going to be quite different. For one, there would be no VFW send-off ceremony, and no more physical exams; only refusing induction remained.

Back through the two sets of glass doors, I once again stepped to the counter, except the enlisted man there was different from the day before. My words, however, were the same. I was there to refuse induction. Giving him my name, I said I had already been through most of the processing, if he could just tell me how I was to refuse. As startled as the first man, he too disappeared into the next room to find out.

Meanwhile, I overheard two of the staff talking in the hall ahead; they were laughing about the threats of disruption the center had received the day before, some students in Morgantown, including a draftee, planning an assault. They noted with some satisfaction that it had not materialized; I was tempted to tell them it might yet, if I knew Frank.

Before long, the enlisted man reappeared with a sergeant. In his early fifties and impressively uniformed with medals, buttons, ribbons and stripes, the sergeant was undoubtedly a "lifer." I suspected that, years ago, he could not wait to enlist on his eighteenth birthday. A lean man, five feet ten, and with a crew cut and a drill sergeant's demeanor, he directed me to his desk in a room off the hall to the right. That morning though, there were few others in the room making our business intimate and all the more uncomfortable.

Was it loathing which kept the sergeant's words to a minimum as he filled out papers for the refusal? He did not look at me the whole time; then again, I did not look at him either. We knew we were from different planets.

After I signed the papers, we went to the office of a lieutenant, a psychologist as it turned out. A man not much older than me, he looked to be a graduate of the Reserve Officer Training Corps. Clean cut and wholesome, he brought back memories of compulsory ROTC when I was a freshman and sophomore. For most of us, it was something between an inconvenience and a joke, those going into the advanced program considered weird.

Initially, we liked ROTC because of the uniforms, everyone curious to see what he looked like in one. I thought I looked pretty good, as I was sure the others did. Doing this fulfilled the soldier fantasy we all had as little boys in our militarized society.

Typical of American parents of the time, my father and mother fed into it; when I put on the ROTC uniform, my father saluted, and my mother looked on proudly. But to me, it as only a fantasy, an illusion. Consequently, it scared me when I discovered some of the other guys taking it very, very seriously.

But now then, what was I to make of this lieutenant? He seemed harmless enough, and in his mild manner he simply asked why I wanted to refuse. I went on to explain about my conscientious objection, albeit after five minutes it was apparent he was not really interested; he only wanted to see whether I was crazy or on drugs. As I was neither, he signed his part of the papers, and directed me to another office where I was left alone for some time.

There were no lights on in the room, only a modest few rays of daylight filtering through mostly closed venetian blinds; it reminded me of the State Director's office. Whether it was this flashback or my nervous perspiration, I was suddenly feeling quite chilly. Just then though, in walked another officer, a captain, his round, honest-looking face making you want him as your bookkeeper. He turned out to be the commander of the induction center, although he seemed a bit young for that.

"Hello," I said, not sure whether I should stand.

As he set my paperwork on his desk and sat down he said, "I'm not here to talk you out of doing this. I'm sure you've given it a great deal of thought. Simply, it is my duty to inform you that refusing induction is a federal offense. I am required to report your refusal to the Selective Service, who in turn will report it to the Justice Department for prosecution. You do understand that, don't you?"

"Yes," I said looking up. "You have to do what you have to do, just as I am doing what I have to do."

As I watched him sign his part of the papers, I was struck by the incongruity—here was this very courteous, pleasant person, a nice guy, signing papers he knew would probably send me to prison. How could I not feel sad as I watched his pen cross the page, much as I felt sad at the lieutenant's and the sergeant's signings. Again the word "illusion" came to mind;

with their uniforms, ranks, commands, procedures and jargon there was something unreal about the military. Then again, I supposed they had to have those things in order to do what they did: wage war, kill people and send those who refused to cooperate off to jail.

The plush, narrow ceremony room, designed as it was for three rows of inductees, had a low stage at the front where stood the captain, the lieutenant, and the sergeant. I stood where I assumed I was to be, choosing the inconspicuous last position in the back row; I did not intend, nor was it in my personality to make a scene, though I noticed the trio keeping a steady eye on me. I wondered, as I looked at all the other young men, whether the three on the stage assumed that with the psychological pressure of the setting and the group, I would relent. I believed the draft board and these three thought I would. Probably in the past, some like me had. On the other hand, I could not help but feel that this scene was rare; West Virginia was not known for draft resistance. In that way, I felt oddly proud as one of the few: " . . . one of the few, the proud," but not a Marine.

The captain explained we were about to enter military service, that he would say the words "United States Army," following which everyone would say his name, and step forward; doing so constituted induction. I reminded myself it was not too late, that I could save myself enormous trouble by just taking that one step. Everyone would understand; no one would hold it against me. Submitting was the norm. In fact, there were those, including some in my own family who would feel relieved. In their eyes, by taking that step I would prove to be a "patriot" after all. I would be no different than them, given their own reservations about the killing in Vietnam. And like them, I would have concluded that the government knew more about the situation over there, and was doing what was right. For them, it would be the loyal thing to do to submit.

These thoughts were all well and good except for one thing, they were not true. I was not like everybody else; I did not believe what the government was doing was right, anymore than I believed that blind loyalty was a good enough reason to allow oneself to be inducted into an organization that killed people. Indeed if there was loyalty to be had, it was me to my conscience.

Just then I heard the captain's words, "United States Army," followed by all the voices, and the single clump forward. My mouth moved with all the others, but it was not my name I said. "I refuse," were my words, my feet remaining firmly planted.

Just as everyone looked to see why I had not moved, the sergeant barked, "Left face!" Some of the farm boys, those who had not had the benefit of compulsory ROTC, turned only their heads to the left, rather than their whole bodies. It would be the last time they made that mistake.

But soon they were organized and marching to the lead of the sergeant, leaving me alone still facing the captain, and the lieutenant. But it was done now, wasn't it? There was nothing left for anyone to say. Walking past me, the captain said I was free to go; the lieutenant, meanwhile, smiled in apparent amazement.

The act itself was simple enough; indeed, the whole affair took less than 40 minutes. To say I was a proud felon would be close to it, proud of myself for seeing it through. But mostly, I was a satisfied felon. I had denied the war its fuel, albeit one drop; if it continued to rage, I knew it was not because of me. Its perpetuation was the doing of the captain, lieutenant, sergeant, the draft board, and all the others in our society who blindly followed the government line. And those who did not? For my part, I now felt in a different league; I had just earned my first stripe.

# CHAPTER FIVE

## THE UNITED STATES OF AMERICA VERSUS DONALD LAIRD SIMONS

In Paris, the peace talks remained at a stalemate at the 42nd weekly session. Meanwhile, the army disclosed the names of First Lieutenant William L. Calley and Staff Sergeant David Mitchell as those responsible for the gunning down of at least 109 men, women and children in the South Vietnamese hamlet of My Lai. Apparently, they entered the village believing it a Viet Cong stronghold, causing them to round up and massacre everyone. Then they worked their way back through the village systematically shooting anything that moved. What next?!

A massive new peace demonstration was next. The November 15, 1969 March on Washington to End the War in Vietnam was organized by David Dellinger, chairman of the National Mobilization Committee to End the War in Vietnam (MOBE). Working with him was Sam Brown, a key organizer of the recent Moratorium Day, and head of a diverse, campus-based coalition. Reorganized as the *New* Mobilization to End the War in Vietnam, they sponsored the November event together.

To appreciate the 1969 March on Washington involves understanding something of its evolution. During its December 1964 national council meeting, Students for a Democratic Society almost inadvertently decided to sponsor an antiwar march in Washington. The initial proposal brought little enthusiasm, but the idea finally won out when it was agreed that anything which brought SDS publicity was worthwhile. Within five weeks, things solidified, albeit in ways not totally anticipated. President Johnson had ordered the bombing of North Vietnam and a general escalation of the war, which immediately raised the ire of liberals. Suddenly, endorsements of the march began arriving from militants and liberals alike, and from individuals as well as groups.

So it was that the first major anti-Vietnam War demonstration in Washington took place on Saturday, April 17, 1965 with an amazing 20,000 attending. Students were the bulk of the crowd, at least 50 colleges sent delegations. The majority were middle class and white, neatly dressed and clean, with few hints of the rage, which would characterize later SDS rallies.[24]

A 1967 antiwar rally in Washington was sponsored by a coalition of peace groups called, as mentioned earlier, the National Mobilization Committee to End the War in Vietnam; however, the MOBE was unable to compromise differences within the coalition over whether the demonstration should be peaceful or disruptive. Finally, they resolved the dilemma by announcing it would be a "do-your-own-thing" event. Accordingly, on Saturday morning October 21, 1967, 50,000 people descended on the Lincoln Memorial; again, most were students. In some ways, it looked like an intercollegiate jamboree, with banners flying from schools such as Harvard, the University of Chicago, the University of Texas, among others; absent were middle-aged couples and clergymen prominent in later rallies.

Also present on this occasion was a profusion of police and military, especially at the Pentagon, which was to be the focus of more confrontational activities later in the day. Indeed, with the conclusion of the Lincoln Memorial program, more than half of the participants crossed the Arlington Memorial Bridge into Virginia, as the more militant faction, mostly identified with the SDS, took over.

A front line of about 1,000 demonstrators confronted the Military Police and federal marshals guarding the Pentagon, the remainder positioning themselves at various points

24. Viorst, p. 395.

around the grounds. About 25 protesters actually slipped through the line of MPs, only to be arrested inside. As night fell, most of the crowd dispersed, although a few hundred spent the night. The next day, the number grew again to approximately 2,000.

Some taunted the soldiers who guarded the entrances, while others offered them food and flowers. Several of the demonstrators were beaten by federal marshals, until finally at midnight on Sunday, those remaining were ordered to leave, which most did. Among those arrested was author Norman Mailer. Military officials put arrest figures for the two days at 647, a very large number for that period.[25]

The 1969 New MOBE-Moratorium march was designed to be peaceful and dignified, while allowing for some militant activity peripherally, especially the night before the main event. As it was, there were an estimated 250,000 marchers, some responsible estimates putting it at twice that number. The target, of course, was President Nixon, the continuing war now his responsibility.

But Nixon did not seem much interested in the protest, a government spokesman saying the thousands who took to the streets to end the war were only a small number compared to those who stayed at home to support the President's policy of gradual withdrawal. Reportedly, Nixon was watching a football game on television the afternoon of November 15, a gesture making the march appear quite meaningless. However, memoirs of White House staff subsequently revealed that Nixon did, in fact, closely monitor the demonstrations, and the football story was given to the press to demoralize the demonstrators.

My recollections of the 1969 March begin with the weather and the long drive. Cold and gray, it rained off and on for our four-hour drive to DC. At least it was not snowing; we all wanted a good turn out. On entering Washington, our immediate problem was finding a place to park. So many vehicles came into Washington that there was nothing downtown near the march site; so, we had to settle on a side street many blocks away. We could then catch a bus, we thought, only we

25. Viorst, p. 414; *New York Times*, October 23, 1967, p. 1.

quickly found those too were filled to capacity. We worried that the day's events would be over before we got there. However, the problem proved less than we thought, a flash of the peace sign stopping a van full of fellow marchers, who made room. Indeed, this concern and spontaneity seemed to be everywhere.

At the staging area, west of 3rd Street Northwest, we noticed security forces were not nearly as visible as in previous antiwar marches. Considerable criticism arose during the 1967 March when riot-trained paratroopers, military police, United States marshals, DC police, National Guardsmen, and the 82nd Airborne were out in the open; Washington looked like a city under martial law.

The key word though was *visible*, as no sooner had we reached the mall, than a huge wave of DC police on motorscooters roared past, only to disappear into an underground tunnel; there was no guessing who or what else was down there. And there was other intimidation; on a rooftop, just beyond a statue of the liberator Simon Bolivar, I spotted a machine gun nest manned by soldiers in combat gear.

The peace march began at 11:00 a.m., winding through the city, past businesses, apartments, and government buildings. At one point a marcher gestured toward a balcony, murmurs of "John Mitchell," the current Attorney General, floating through the crowd; true enough, there stood a man smoking a pipe who looked like Mitchell, but it was hard to be certain from that distance. It was not unlike the rumor later in the day that some had seen President Nixon meeting with a group of the demonstrators.

As we continued along, I was surprised there were not more spectators lining the streets; there were some, but for a demonstration that size, I expected more. It then occurred to me that fear kept people away, fear of violence. But the marchers feared it too, huddling close as we moved stiffly down the middle of the wide streets.

What encouraged me most was the number of adults in the ranks this time. In our section were clergy of all denominations, and the parents of soldiers alive and dead. It was the adults, even more than the young people, who had their arms linked in a show of solidarity against the war.

That I was doing what I could in my way, was also true of the young man behind the voice coming to my shoulder. "What are the odds of it?" he said, my turning to see if it was who I thought it was. "What are the odds of seeing someone else from Morgantown in a crowd of half a million people?"

"It's good to see you, Frank," I said, noting his weary, disheveled look, as though he had been up demonstrating all night, which he told me he had.

The more militant rally, which kept Frank up all night, included a march on the South Vietnamese embassy intended as a challenge to the legitimacy of the Saigon government. There was a confrontation with riot police that erupted into violence resulting in the gassing, beating, and arresting of many of the 2–3,000 participants.

Not quite sure what to say, I began to ask him about his draft status, when he unexpectedly remarked, "You know, Don, if either of us deserves to be rid of his draft problems, it's you. Good luck."

I was sure he wanted to be rid of his too, as I shook his hand and wished him luck as well. Still, I could not help but think it an irony that part of our previous relationship was as combatants in junior high school and again in college. We once wrestled for the championship in an all-school tournament; and in college, we were toe-to-toe in Shodokan karate. Now here we were on the same side, warriors for peace.

It grew progressively damper and colder as the day wound down, but our group persevered for the last of the speeches and the songs at the Washington Monument. Suddenly, a depression overtook me, I felt very much alone. Faded was the emotional high from refusing induction, returning the uncertainty and anxiety over what was ahead. As we raised the peace sign and swayed our arms back and forth to John Lennon's song "Give Peace a Chance," it was all I could do to contain my emotion.

The truth was, my draft problems now felt out of control; I was afraid. It was great that all these people were marching, listening to speeches and singing, but when it was all done, when the event was over, most would go home and get back to leading normal lives. And that included the several friends standing beside me; they would go back to their classes and the Cafe, and yes, talk for weeks now about how inspiring Washington was.

But not me. I had to look forward to being arrested. Then everyone would say "Where's Don tonight?" or "I just saw him the other day." "He was at the march, wasn't he?" All the while, I would be behind bars. No, when I left the March on Washington, I knew I had only more anxiety, paranoia and fear to look forward to. And they would all be mine, and mine alone.

I was feeling sorry for myself. In my personal confrontation with the draft I lost sight of its effect on my entire generation. For the minute, the enormity of the situation escaped me. Some 30 million young men came of age during the Vietnam era. All of them, in one degree or another, had to come to terms with the Selective Service System and the limited choices: enter the military, qualify for an exemption, refuse and be imprisoned, or leave the country. No, I was not alone, but the closer it got to being me against my government, the more my focus narrowed on the personal nature of this struggle.

Also discouraging was the public perception of the demonstration, as the violence between the government forces and the more militant factions dominated the news. Attorney General Mitchell said it reminded him of scenes of the Russian Revolution. Less partisan observers were no less dismayed, the violent clash with the government being how some in the country perceived the antiwar movement generally.

I was greatly frustrated by the media's limited reporting of the event and wrote a letter-to-the-editor of the local newspaper:

This is to express my extreme disappointment in the two Sunday *Dominion-Post* articles on the "March on Washington" peace demonstration. I was angered to see that the two articles scarcely mentioned the 250,000–500,000 peaceful Americans who participated in the main November 15 march.

Being there, I know I was deeply impressed by the mass of people. Never before in the history of America have so many marched in Washington for the end to war, though for some reason that was not considered newsworthy. Never before have there been such profound feelings of brotherhood concentrated in one place for the cause of peace, also not considered newsworthy. Never before have so many expressed such confidence in a war-free future; but a warless tomorrow was also not newsworthy.

Instead, the *Dominion-Post* reporters chose to highlight the discomforts we all experienced, and the unrepresentative militant activity. That they felt was newsworthy. That was what they believed people wanted to read, and what the editor accepted as representative of the Washington event.

I am certainly disappointed, and would indicate there was far more to the "March on Washington" than you reported.

Two weeks later the government announced a lottery system for the draft, the first since 1942. Except in the case of a national emergency, draft liability would end for those not called by any given year end.

Despite appearances, the lottery did not just come out of the clear blue. In 1966, struck by the apparent inequities of the current draft law, Democratic Senator Ted Kennedy of Massachusetts proposed reinstituting a lottery. It was not until 1969, however, that the new lottery was implemented as a response to growing war resistance and to address the complaints of registrants who could not make career, marriage, or other plans while their draft status remained uncertain.

To put it in historical context, the Selective Service Act of 1948 was amended and extended by an Act of Congress on June 19, 1951. Title I of that Act, called the Universal Military Training and Service Act, was the authority under which the Selective Service System operated. In 1963 the Act was extended four years, and again in 1967, when its name was changed to the Military Selective Service Act of 1967. In that same year, Congress established a prohibition against a lottery, which in 1969 it repealed, making way for the first lottery since World War II.

The random drawing included all 366 calendar dates and the 26 letters of the alphabet. The calendar dates corresponded to the birth dates of the pool of 19 to 26 year olds. The order in which men would be called depended upon the randomly drawn dates and letters.

Men with birth dates among the first third selected were given a "good" chance of being called, those in the middle an "uncertain" chance, and those in the last third a "poor chance." Draft liability was for one year. Future lotteries were slated for each fall to incorporate the new pool of 19 year olds.

Because deferments, including college, occupational and hardship cases were continued, one still had the draft to worry about when a deferment ended, albeit he would know by then his chances of being called; that is, those deferred were to retain the priority they had in the pool when their names were returned at the end of their deferment.

The government line was that this system would be fairer, as all 19 to 26 year olds had an equal chance of being called. The lottery was also a direct attempt to quell campus unrest and silence criticism that a disproportionate number of blacks and other minorities were being drafted.

While the lottery satisfied those for whom racial imbalance in the draft was the primary issue, it did not defuse the peace movement. Indeed, the peace movement continued to grow. The government's attempt to shift the focus from the war failed. What fueled the fires of resistance was not *who* was being sent to fight, but why this nation was fighting at all.

As for me, if I envied those who would now know the likelihood of being drafted during just one year of liability, it was with the knowledge that if I had the same luxury, my antiwar position and activity would have been the same. Even if I had been exempt due to the lottery, I still would have worked to end the war, attended Moratorium Day and marched on Washington.

January 1970 was bitterly cold in Morgantown, indeed throughout the east. I was now living in a tiny apartment behind a laundromat where the rent was free to the person overseeing it. My life at that time consisted of finishing my Master's thesis, working at the University Book Store, doing my duties at the laundromat, and wondering when I would be arrested. My daily routine included: unlocking the laundromat at 7:00 a.m., being at the bookstore at 9:00 a.m., working until 5:00 p.m., writing my thesis in the evening, checking in with friends at the Cafe around 10:00 p.m., closing the laundromat at midnight, back to the Cafe to conclude the visit with friends, back to the laundromat at 1:00 a.m. to mop the floors and clean the machines, in bed by 2:00 a.m., up again at 7:00.

This structured routine helped me control the new levels of anxiety I was feeling; also helpful was the unexpected return of optimism which had me convinced the local board now saw I was serious and would reconsider my CO application.

The demonstration of my resolve did affect how family and friends responded to me. Understandably, my parents were now very worried. On the other hand, the Cafe people seemed perplexed, almost as if they did not think I would go this far; I was treated with a new found respect. Yet, we all suffered from a feeling of helplessness, including the sense that all anyone could do was stand there and watch me go down in flames, the government having all the matches.

On the morning of January 22, I was beginning my routine, not without noting how cold it remained. Combating the sub-zero temperatures had me near asphyxiation all week, as the small gas heater in the uninsulated apartment and the four burners of the kitchen stove were my sole sources of heat. Fortunately, I had enough sense to leave a window ajar near the top of the ten-foot ceiling; I also opened the one exterior door from time to time for fresh air. But how long could you leave the door open when it was 10 below zero outside?

Unlocking the laundromat that morning, I began my trudge down Falling Run Road toward the bookstore, the icy wind freezing my face. A long walk in the best of conditions, it could not end too soon that morning.

My job at the store consisted of unpacking and shelving textbooks, showing students where to find things, and sending books and materials to surrounding schools. I was well thought of there, always on time and easy to get along with. I told some co-workers of my draft problems, and while they did not necessarily share my antiwar views, neither did they want to see me in trouble. "Good luck," they would say. "Good luck."

It was just this response which underscored the loneliness of my struggle. Would these same people stand by as their neighbor was hauled off to some concentration camp? "Good luck," I imagined they would wave. "Good luck."

When I took the bookstore job the previous fall I did not reveal any of this to the cool, business-like woman manager, though I alerted her to the possibility of authorities coming to see me on a personal matter. So it was that just after noon on January 22, while I was working on some shelves in the back, the manager, looking pale, confronted me. "The gentlemen you've been expecting are here," she said, with a gesture toward her office.

I thought I was prepared for it, but how do you prepare? In the office, an FBI agent, and a U.S. marshal showed their identification, the former asking if I was Donald Simons, which he knew already. He then presented a document which read, "The United States of America vs. Donald Laird Simons. The Grand Jury charges . . ." It was very humbling. In a way I felt honored; but also intimidated, which I was sure I was supposed to feel. The U.S. marshal then read me my rights.

He informed me I would be spared the handcuffs if I came along quietly; he said they did not want to embarrass me unnecessarily in front of my co-workers. As we walked through the store though, my co-workers were nowhere to be seen. Perhaps they were unaware of what was happening.

Outside was an unmarked government car, the U.S. marshal and I climbing into the back, while the FBI agent sat up front with another marshal. In a moment we were winding our way through campus. It was quite incredible, my looking out at all the familiar buildings, sites of my classes and places that brought back both fond and difficult memories. And here I was *arrested*, three law enforcement agents around me.

And silent agents at that, except for the occasional casual comment among themselves, mainly about the driving conditions. The FBI agent was the friendliest, and seemed the least like a lawman. Under six feet tall and stocky, his conservative glasses made him look quite the intellectual.

The marshal beside me seemed friendly too, but in a hard way. No doubt it was from all the years of transporting convicts between jails. He looked 10 years older than the FBI man, though he probably was not; I suspected him to be quite capable of violence. The marshal at the wheel was heavier, sitting like a lump at the controls, left shoulder half-cocked, and against the door. Middle-aged, he remained expressionless, and all but wordless, the whole trip. Actually, he seemed bored by it all.

It was not a long drive to the county jail, but what a peculiar feeling as the car turned the corner at High Street and Chancery Row. Looking up at the clock tower, then down at the plaza of the Courthouse Square, I could still picture myself standing there in the crowd on Moratorium Day. Little did I know back then, as I listened to the speeches and my eyes surveyed the scene, that this was where and how the next episode would play out.

Fingerprinting was the first order of business at the jail, a procedure and place I was familiar with from an experience in my youth. My father was one of the organizers of a community program that taught youth about law enforcement; once we took a tour of the jail conducted by the county sheriff. I never suspected that someday I would be an arrestee and experience what they demonstrated to us that day.

While I remembered little about fingerprinting, the jail made a lasting impression. Above all I was struck by how hard everything looked, no pillows, curtains, or carpet, not even globes over the glaring overhead lights. No warm colors. The floors were gray, the walls dark red brick, the cage-like cells of black steel bars, the wire-reinforced opaque windows opening out to more bars, and the view across the street another brick wall. And everywhere the smell of disinfectant, mixed as it was on that occasion with liver frying in the kitchen below.

Here I was standing against the wall outside a row of those same cells, a height marker at my back. There were two deputy sheriffs in front of me who, at the moment, were having a terrible time with the jail's camera. The inordinate shaking of one of them led me to believe he thought I was a dangerous criminal; one false move and I was sure he would shoot me on the spot. I learned later that Frank had also been arrested that day, which might have explained the jumpiness.

As it happened, the same FBI agent and two federal marshals had been looking for Frank earlier that day, and not finding him, went to his father's place of work. Unwilling to reveal the whereabouts of his son, Frank's father was then threatened. With this, the agent and marshals decided to go after me.

In the meantime, Frank's father notified his son of what had happened, whereupon Frank contacted a deputy sheriff acquaintance, who confirmed that there was a warrant for his arrest. Later that evening, after the agent and marshals were finished with me, they went back for Frank, who surrendered to them; he spent the night in a neighboring county jail.

I continued to watch as the two deputies fumbled with the camera. Saying my father had one just like it, I finally stepped forward at great personal risk with a suggestion, "Perhaps if you reset the shutter. . . ." In another moment, the picture was taken.

A jail cell was next, I was sure. To my surprise, however, I was led to an office across the street, where the FBI man, with one of the U.S. marshals standing guard in the hall, asked if I would like to call an attorney, or at least to call home. I thought that was an excellent idea. It was 4:00 p.m., and my father would probably be home by then. But on phoning, my mother was the only one there. I explained what had happened, and what the FBI man had said—if bond could be posted before five o'clock, I would not have to spend the night in jail.

My mother, a worrier as it was, did not want to hear about arrest and jail, although I had warned her of the probability. Because my draft resistance was something she did not fully understand or appreciate, much less a matter she felt she had any control over, her reaction was purely that of a mother. With anxiety in her voice she explained that my father had left his office, but had to run errands, so she did not know precisely when he would be home. But she would send him the moment he walked in the door. I could hear her pulse in the receiver, or was it mine?

So now it was a waiting game, my having 45 minutes to squirm, and with no idea where my father was, or whether he would get there in time. All I could do was sit patiently on the hardwood bench, the grim, drab office looking more so in the fading afternoon light. All the while, in the hall outside, the

FBI agent and the U.S. marshal engaged in unexpectedly jocular conversation. Across from me a bureaucrat sat expressionless, filling out paperwork presumably on my behalf. Only one remark was made to me for the next 30 minutes, the FBI man asking, "What's a good kid like you doing in this mess?" The question had occurred to me too; I was tempted to tell him it was just that "goodness" that had me there.

Sitting there on the bench, I recalled an experience in that same building six months earlier, when on filing for conscientious objector status I sought letters of support. My father suggested I visit our family attorney, a former State Senator, and a man well-known in the community; a letter from him would carry some weight. Indeed, when I entered his office he was very cordial, asking how my parents were, to which I responded how happy I was to meet him after hearing his name in our household over the years. But when we sat down and I began describing how I had filed for conscientious objector status with the Selective Service, his eyes quickly became like ice.

He asked the basis of my conscientious objection, which I explained in a halting fashion, because it was obvious he had no intention of supporting me; instead, I sensed he considered me one of the enemy. This was not to say we argued. There was nothing to argue about; he was right and I was wrong. A young man went into the army when he was called, regardless. It was one's patriotic duty. On subsequent encounters, for example when I saw him on the street, he would only shake his head and say, "Where did your parents go wrong?" My father was embarrassed when I told him what had happened. After years, it was the end of his relationship with that lawyer.

But now it was five o'clock. Incarceration seemed certain. To his credit, the FBI man asked the clerk for 15 more minutes, circumstances being what they were. The U.S. marshal yawned; he wanted to go home. But come 5:30, we all looked at each other. Was not the effort lost? However, as I stood to be led out, in walked my father.

As our eyes met I was reminded what it was to have a father, someone to come to your rescue when you got into something over your head. Unlike when I was a little kid, when there might be a small smile as he rescued me from a confrontation with a bigger kid, this time there was no smile. He and I both knew that the bigger kid I was arguing with now was the United States government, and while he might be able to retrieve me this one time, it was only going to get worse. Consequently, not much was said as he gave me a ride back to my laundromat apartment. He knew he could not tell me to stop following my heart, or to turn a deaf ear to my conscience. So the sum of our words were "Thanks, dad," and "Goodnight, son."

That night my little uninsulated, hole-in-the-wall apartment felt like the Waldorf.

I now needed a trial attorney. My first choice was the draft counselor-lawyer in Pittsburgh; he was the natural choice. He was familiar with the case, sympathetic, and an expert in draft law and Selective Service Rules and Regulations.

Sitting in his modest downtown office, frozen Fifth Avenue glistening below, I detailed what had happened since we had last talked in October. Finally I blurted, "Would you represent me in court?" I was sure he would; he need only say yes. When he said no, my face fell. He explained it was not for lack of interest or support, but quite simply he was not licensed to practice in the state of West Virginia; he would, however, help in whatever other way he could.

Back home I nervously thumbed through the yellow pages, only to close them; attorneys in my town, I was certain, would have nothing to do with me. However, I noted in the local newspaper coverage of our arrests there was mention of Frank's attorney. Of course, Frank would need one too. Not finding the man listed in the local directory, I tried my father's faculty directory. Sure enough, he was a law professor. I phoned him.

An enthusiastic black man, the lawyer had apparently sent word to Frank through a common friend that he would be willing to represent him without charge because of Frank's commitment to civil rights. He was also a Vietnam veteran. In my matter, however, he said that unfortunately, he could not possibly take another draft case and still meet his responsibilities to the university. On the other hand, he had heard of a man in Charleston whom he understood to be strongly against the war, and who might be interested. Again I picked up the phone.

# THE U.S. VERSUS DONALD LAIRD SIMONS

The last time I had driven to the state capital, it was to see the Selective Service State Director; the man I met on this trip stood at the other end of the spectrum. Tall and distinguished, to my surprise he had white hair, what there was of it, and well-worn eyes; the phone had not revealed his age. Yet, he had practiced law in West Virginia and the surrounding states for over 50 years, and had defended several landmark cases. He had even argued before the United States Supreme Court. He had twice received a prestigious award from the Secretary of State of West Virginia, and had published numerous commentaries in a leading Charleston newspaper; I was impressed.

Furthermore, he also seemed an expert, and an ally. "You know," he said, "nowhere in the Constitution does it authorize the drafting of United States citizens to fight in foreign countries. The Constitution provides only for 'the common defense,' and Vietnam has not invaded the United States. Also, the United Nations Charter, to which we are a signatory power, prohibits interference in the internal affairs of an independent foreign country where that country has not threatened the other country. Vietnam has not threatened us. They are having a civil war which is none of our business."

"And we're over there killing thousands of their people," I said.

"That's what I like about your case, and admire about you. This war is a moral issue as much as a legal one, and if what we are doing over there is a moral catastrophe, it is no less so here at home where it is tearing our country apart. I'm a veteran and a member of the American Legion, but above all I'm a Christian. No good Christian can stand by and allow this atrocity to continue."

"In addition to Christianity, I have studied Eastern religions and greatly respect that spiritual point of view," I then said. "And I'll tell you, when I saw pictures of the Vietnamese Buddhist monks setting themselves on fire as a protest to the war, it broke my heart."

"I saw those pictures too," he replied. "The Buddhists were protesting a lot of things." He paused. "You have a challenging case here, Mr. Simons, not the least of which is the injustice done to you by your local draft board in denying you conscientious objector status. That they have forced you to the point of prosecution is a travesty. I believe we have an excellent chance of winning."

Yet, as we shook hands as lawyer and client, something was bothering me. I worried that here was a guy, albeit successful and well-known, but a man on the down side of his career. For all I knew, he had not had a substantial case in some time, perhaps seeing me as a chance for one last hurrah. Partly substantiating this was a subsequent letter:

Dear Donald:

Yesterday I mailed to you a first draft of a couple of motions I wish to file on your behalf, if satisfactory to you.

Could either you or your father or mother see if one of the History or Political Science professors will be able and willing to verify allegations with regard to the CIA's activities in Vietnam, and also efforts of Catholics to take over the religion of the country from the Buddhists, which resulted for a while in a number of immolations of Buddhists.

P.S. Also, do you believe the members of the religious organization to which you belong and are a minister would be willing to contribute to your expenses in carrying your case, if need be, to the Supreme Court of the United States?

It certainly sounded like a last hurrah to me. Finally, I settled on the rather obvious point that I was retaining my lawyer, not the other way around; I was resolved not to let him turn my case into more than I was prepared to handle. Accordingly, I sent him a letter outlining the approach I preferred, namely one that stressed draft board procedural errors in denying my conscientious objector status.

Several days later I received a letter from my attorney backing off his position slightly and agreeing to try my approach first. Even so, he emphasized that his approach and issues were equally important and must be included for a complete defense. I appreciated his desire to put the war on trial, and believed it was to his credit. But the truth was, at this point, I was afraid and just wanted to get this over.

# CHAPTER SIX
## EYE TO EYE WITH SAM

On the date I was to be arraigned, my lawyer made an oral motion in court to remand my case for appeal to the Selective Service State Appeal Board, citing examples of procedural irregularities by the local board. The U.S. Attorney was required to respond to this motion within 10 days.

On March 19, the government submitted an eight-page motion detailing relevant draft law and why I was previously denied, and was still not eligible for, an appeal to the Appeal Board.

In response, my attorney put together a list of legal reasons countering the government's argument. Sending me a copy he wrote, "I believe this should relieve your anxiety about your case, and eliminate any further need to consult the Pittsburgh people."

I did not like that. I reminded him it was my draft counselor's list of procedural errors, *his* input, which had us in what appeared to be a favorable position. I further pointed out to my lawyer that he had not used the full list in his counter argument, and that I would be just as happy if he submitted it all; I wanted a quick resolution. To mind were my draft counselor's words that going to court was not to our advantage. Several days later, my attorney wrote: "I will call the additional facts to the attention of the district attorney, and am confident he will voluntarily dismiss the indictment."

In response to the government's written argument, my attorney filed a nine-page "Motion to Nolle the Indictment," which read in part:

The Order of the Draft Board which the indictment alleges defendant disobeyed was illegal and void because it ordered him to report for induction into the Armed Forces for service in an undeclared war. The Tonkin Gulf Resolution was invalid, especially as construed and applied. The President of the United States has no authority to make commitments, which come within the treaty making power, without the advise and consent of the Senate before they become effective. The war in Vietnam, Laos, Cambodia and Thailand is not in defense of the United States. None of those countries gave us any casus belli. The Preamble to our Constitution states that the United States government was formed to provide for the common defense of the States, not offense. The Tenth Amendment to the U.S. Constitution states that powers not delegated by it to the United States government are reserved to the States and the people thereof. Nowhere does the Constitution authorize Congress to draft American men and boys to be sent as mercenary soldiers to fight for Vietnam or any other country than the United States. The Thirteenth Amendment to the U.S. Constitution provides that involuntary servitude, except as a punishment for crime whereof the party shall have been duly convicted, shall not exist within the United States, or any place subject to their jurisdiction.

This was the crux of his argument for taking the case to the Supreme Court.

Meanwhile, in Washington D.C., more than 50,000 people turned out for a march and rally calling for "victory in Vietnam," an event organized by a right-wing, fundamentalist preacher; the marchers carried signs and chanted quotations from Scripture.

In an effort to renew the Moratorium movement, a series of demonstrations were held across the nation on April 15th. The date was chosen to underscore the link between higher taxes and war expenditures. Participation was small compared to the October 15, 1969 Moratorium Day, but there was considerably more violence.[26]

26. *New York Times*, April 16, 1970, p. 1; April 17, 1970, p. 42.

Elsewhere, Governor James A. Rhodes ordered national guard troops onto the Ohio State campus during two days of student disorder in which 600 were arrested and 20 were reportedly wounded by police shotgun fire. At about the same time, President Nixon told a nationwide television audience that he had ordered American troops into action against Communist sanctuaries up to 20 miles inside Cambodia. In an explosive reaction to this, many campuses across the nation erupted into violent clashes between students and police. A confrontation between national guardsmen and over 500 students at Kent State University ended in death for four young people after the guardsmen fired a volley into the crowd. In the meantime, the Paris peace talks entered their third year, as delegates met for the 66th session. The North Vietnamese had canceled an earlier session to protest the American drive into Cambodia.

Soon after, I witnessed something on the campus of our university I never thought I would see. In response to the May 4th incident at Kent State, a group of students held a memorial vigil. It grew slowly, until by the next day, there were hundreds of students congregated at the heart of the campus. The demonstration included an assault on the university president's office; he was targeted because of his refusal to condemn the Cambodian invasion and the Kent State killings.

Carrying a mock coffin containing an effigy, the demonstrators marched to the administration building, where they demanded entry. Finally, three from the crowd were permitted a meeting with members of the school administration; but none of the members would issue a statement on the president's behalf, or endorse the students' position. In anger, the protesters returned to the streets where they burned the coffin and effigy.

All the while, local traffic through campus was at a standstill. "We're staying in the streets because we're not satisfied with the bullshit we're getting from the university," shouted one demonstrator. "The streets belong to the people," yelled another. A few faculty members seemed to agree; the chairman of the philosophy department argued, "We've got to protect ourselves against repression." Believing student dissidents were fair game for the "bootlicking pigs," the professor

99

announced he was canceling his final exams and giving his students "A" grades for the semester.

That evening the protesters dispersed, only to have the local newspaper editorialize, "It's to the great credit to all concerned that the violence-inviting radicals did not succeed in creating a general riot and tragedy." It trusted that the town and the university would keep its cool. Noting the foul language of the demonstrators, the paper went on to urge university authorities to determine who the "law-insulting riot seekers" were and expel them.

That evening, the school's Director of University Relations further clarified the president's position saying that the head of the administration would meet with no one under the threat of coercion, that indeed his making an appearance at that time might actually trigger a riot. The official added that the president "doesn't normally issue statements on socio-political issues, because in the public's mind, his views inevitably become those of the university. West Virginia University belongs to all the people of West Virginia who hold diverse views." He repeated a statement the president issued earlier, that the university would not tolerate disruption of its activities, and apologized to the townspeople for the inconvenience caused by disruption of local traffic.

Yet, that was not the end of it. Following a rally in the downtown area the next day, crowds of students once more flooded the campus, the leaders returned to the administration building and repeated their demands. I watched as they were again turned away. Frustrated, the assemblage moved back into the streets where they continued to disrupt traffic. Just then a group of counter-demonstrators descended from the fraternity houses, and a shouting and shoving match began, things quickly getting out of hand. This was much more than the university and local police could handle, and a request to the governor quickly brought riot-trained state police.

The troopers arrived on campus at 4:40 in the afternoon and announced they would be clearing the streets. Within minutes, a wedge of police ascended in full riot gear, their ventilating gas masks emitting a strange, intimidating buzz. In a steady march, riot batons at the ready, they soon split the crowd, twice passing through the student demonstrators. But the crowd just regrouped behind them, prompting the police to turn and begin tossing tear gas canisters. Putting handkerchiefs over their faces, the students threw the canisters back.

All knew the batons would be next. The police, however, were also apparently trained in negotiation. They interrupted their tactics with an offer of a face-saving compromise; they would depart if the students did the same. Agreed, two massive police buses roared up, the troopers boarded and pulled away as promised. The demonstrators, of course, accepted this as a great victory, whereupon they cheered, jeered, and waved their fists as the buses disappeared down the hill. Then, the students departed, a deal being a deal. From my vantage point on the perimeter of the scene, I could only shake my head. On a traditionally conservative campus like ours, who would believe such a thing could happen? I then reminded myself that I was arrested not 50 feet away just a few months earlier.

Speaking at the University of Pennsylvania, New York Mayor John Lindsay criticized fellow Republican, Vice President Spiro Agnew for his "intemperate language" regarding those taking a stand against the war. He went on to say that he had "unending admiration" for those "heroic" enough to refuse to serve in Vietnam. Referring to Lindsay in a subsequent Washington speech, Agnew expressed his disdain for "men now in power in this country, who do not represent authority, who cannot cope with tradition, and who believe that the people of America are ready to support revolution as long as it is done with a cultured voice and a handsome profile."

Mayor Lindsay's remarks boosted my spirits at a time when I had little to be happy about. With prosecution pending, even the completion of my graduate program was a hollow victory. I was all but obsessed by the case; so much so that friends at the Cafe knew what subject to avoid; they had learned not to ask, "How's the case?" or "When are you going to trial?"

My reaction was like popping the cap off a soda bottle, the frustration, anxiety and disbelief that I was in this predicament, came pouring forth.

"I can't believe they think I'm the enemy!" I would shout to Mac, waving my arms. "Since when is being a peaceful person and refusing to take another human life a criminal offense? Something is really screwed up here!"

"Easy, Don," Mac would say. "I'm on your side."

Still, if some of my friends backing off made me feel more isolated, no less so did my solution to the problem. "Don't ask," I would say when someone looked about to inquire the latest. My morale reached a new low with the news Frank had his charges dropped, a court-ordered psychiatric evaluation resulting in a IV-F disqualification from the service.

It seemed clear the government was looking for an easy way out with Frank, given his recent history of trouble-making; meanwhile, they could use the psychiatric disqualification to identify the more vocal draft resisters as crazy. Then I realized something very important. By making an example of people like me, the more mainstream type, they would send a loud, clear message to the majority that "bucking the system" meant big trouble. It was not in the government's best interest to dispose of me administratively, guys like me should be forced to comply or be sent to jail. Relatively few young people could travel the road Frank did, but the mainstream could identify with me, and that could not be encouraged.

My initial jealousy over Frank being free of the draft quickly changed to happiness for him. I knew how hard he worked, the good he was trying to do and how he suffered with all this. Moreover, Frank's disqualification meant there was one less person the government could use to wage war.

My continuing state of anxiety prompted me to consider the benefits of a complete change of environment, so I decided to spend some time with my parents at their summer house in New Jersey. There I could get some temporary work until it was clear where my case was going. Bags packed, I drove eight hours to the Jersey shore where I found short-term work as a construction laborer, and then as a desk clerk at a motor inn.

Soon after, my attorney called with encouraging news contained in the following court order:

This day the Court having considered defendant's motion to nolle the indictment in the above styled case, and having determined the necessity of additional information before ruling on the motion, it is therefore ORDERED that the United States Attorney for the Northern Judicial District of West Virginia make available to the Court the complete Selective Service file of defendant, Donald Laird Simons.

This was excellent news. Even better was the judge's subsequent determination that there was, in fact, a prima facie case for my conscientious objection, meaning in the absence of evidence to the contrary, my CO claim was valid. Consequently, he ordered the Selective Service to reopen my file for reconsideration of my application. He added that claiming conscientious objection after the issuance of an induction order should not be grounds for denying me CO status.

With great anticipation my lawyer and I awaited news of the local board's reevaluation. In fact, my attorney considered the case all but resolved. All too quickly though, the local board reported:

The board is not convinced by information presented by Mr. Simons that his personal beliefs, views and actions are strong enough to demonstrate the test of sincerity as defined in Section 9 of Local Board Memorandum No. 107 dated July 6, 1970. The Board has reviewed and studied the information presented by Mr. Simons, and it is our opinion by unanimous vote that he be classified I-A.

I was stunned. What did they want?

It occurred to me that the local board, like the demonstrating students back at the university, found themselves in a face-saving situation. Because of their previous errors, they had been ordered by a federal judge to redo what in their minds they had already done correctly. To save face then, their position had to be that their assessment of me was the same as at the outset.

Returning to Morgantown, I went to the local board office to ask what more I could do to convince them of my sincerity. The clerk, however, said all she could do was provide a copy of the complete board report, which was at least something; previously, a registrant was not permitted access to such internal memoranda. It meant I could use the details of the board's rejection for fresh argument.

Being classified I-A again opened the door to new procedural remedies, including an actual personal appearance, not an interview, and if necessary, the long-sought appeal to the State Board. Yet here was the dilemma, should I endure another face-to-face meeting with the local board, recalling that they had consistently rejected me, or should I waive that and appeal directly to the State Board?

I pictured the looks on the faces of the local board members, masks hiding a bias which under the best of circumstances, I wondered if I could penetrate. For all I knew they had never granted the I-O classification. Furthermore, was not their view of me tainted, their minds made up? It seemed to me the case should go to fresh eyes, and to a panel more apt to be impartial.

However, going to the State Board involved a trade off, that is, no face-to-face presentation was permitted; their judgement was based solely on the information in my file. But then, I had a renewed confidence in that file; indeed, had not the judge seen a prima facie case in it? And it now contained a detailed rebuttal to the local board's most recent report. Furthermore, if worse came to worse, one dissenting vote on the state level would send it to the National Appeal Board; by then it would surely occur to the Selective Service that I was sincere and would not submit to induction.

It was then that an unrelated call to my uncle on the West Coast resulted in an offer of work, that is if I did not mind learning the painting trade. I explained to him I might have to leave on the spur of the moment, either for Selective Service or court business, which he accepted. As it turned out even my attorney okayed my leaving; it would probably be three months before the State Appeal Board reported.

Those months out West were lonely. I rented a small bachelor's apartment where I spent most of my hours when not working. I did not own anything, I did not have a car; I had only a bed and a makeshift desk where I filled my time writing depressing entries in a journal. Mostly, I missed my friends at the Cafe, even though I knew that period of my life was over.

I felt in limbo, living in exile in a foreign country. On the one hand, there was a dream-like quality to living there, the surroundings continued to green and to flower long after all back East was lifeless and monochrome. Looking at snow-capped mountains in the distance while wearing a short-sleeved shirt seemed unreal. The laid-back atmosphere invited relaxation; I was tempted to feel safe.

But I was not, and I was quick to remind myself of it, quick to remember safety was not why I was there. I simply had to do something; I had to survive while the draft problem sorted itself out. That it was slow to do so accounted for the knot of frustration and depression continually with me.

Nor did I feel it was something I could talk about with my relatives. Part of the problem was that my uncle, aunt, and two female cousins were what I called "go to" people, which was to say they would do all they could for you, but you had to go to them. The trouble was, by nature I was not a "go to" person, which only compounded my loneliness. Then there was our conflicting views regarding military service, a subject which mercifully, we did not broach. So I painted houses, and on Sundays read the voluminous *Los Angeles Times*, first page to last, closely following the war.

President Nixon was in the news announcing a "major new initiative for peace." Nixon offered the Communists a "cease fire in place," and an international peace conference on all three Indochina states: Vietnam, Cambodia, and Laos. However, the Communists continued their hard line, repeating their demand that the United States withdraw unilaterally.

In other news, the President's Commission on Campus Unrest decried the Kent State University shootings as "unnecessary, unwarranted and inexcusable." At the same time, the panel condemned the actions of some of the student demonstrators as "intolerable" and said the students must share the blame for the killings.

FBI Director J. Edgar Hoover told a Senate subcommittee that an antiwar group headed by the Reverends Daniel and

Philip Berrigan, brothers jailed for destroying draft records, had planned to kidnap a high government official. This official, later identified as Nixon advisor Henry Kissinger, was to be taken in an effort to force a halt to American air raids in Indochina, and to free "political prisoners" at home. Kissinger met with three of the alleged co-conspirators in what he described as a series of weekly "nonpolitical" talks to give "concerned people a sense of being listened to." In other words, he did not want these people to have the impression the government was ignoring them. But "nonpolitical" talks? It seemed unlikely that Kissinger and those working to end U.S. involvement in Vietnam met to talk about the weather.

At the same time, in a daring attempt to rescue American prisoners of war in North Vietnam, 50 American commandos helicoptered into the Sontay POW camp, 23 miles from Hanoi, only to find that the 50–100 captives had been evacuated.

In Paris, the peace talks were again stalemated, January 1971 marking the 100th meeting since the Allies and the Communists began the talks in January of 1969.

Like most in the country I was now numb from the war; the heavy loss of men, women, children and materiel inconceivable, the peace talks a joke, and protest, personal and collective, seemingly futile. Similarly, I became increasingly impatient with my draft problems. I wanted a resolution. Being 2,500 miles from it did not make the least difference; it was constantly on my mind. Finally though, in mid-January I received a letter from my attorney saying the State Appeal Board had made its decision; he was expecting notification within the next few days and would relay the findings the moment he heard.

He also included a description of his activities since last we met. He said a bill had been introduced in the West Virginia State Legislature prohibiting the drafting of West Virginians to serve in Vietnam; Massachusetts had a similar bill. His appearance before the State Senate Judiciary Committee in support of the West Virginia version was to be followed by spots on local television and radio shows.

With his letter came hope that it was all about to end, that after four months with the State Board and nearly four years overall, justice was at hand. I did not feel animosity toward the Selective Service, or bitterness over what had happened; rather, it all seemed to be a comedy of errors to me, procedural errors and errors of judgement by the local board and the State Director; perhaps even communication errors on my part. As for the government players, I doubted they were bad people; they were merely doing what they thought was right. Problems arose though, when it came to priorities. For the Selective Service, and for that matter for the judicial system, the priority was inducting people into the military with the least possible disruption. For me, the priority was morality. The nature of the war in Vietnam put these priorities on a collision course.

The point was, I did not believe the Selective Service was going out of its way to do me an injustice. Perhaps if I were a war veteran sitting on a local draft board, I might also be suspicious of young men unwilling to serve in the army. However, given that bias, I would disqualify myself in CO cases, yielding to more impartial members on the board.

I naively hoped that this sort of impartiality existed at the State Board. Understandably, when their decision finally came I read it with great anticipation.

The judgement was simple enough. They felt the local board was in a better position to determine the sincerity of my claim; they were turning the case back to the lower panel. Moreover, the vote was unanimous by quorum, meaning I would not be permitted further appeal. Immediately, the local board sent a new order for me to report for induction.

I was to appear for induction on February 2nd, with the court requiring me to be present for a pretrial hearing on the third; were they assuming something?

Back in Morgantown an exasperated Donald Simons phoned the local board clerk to say he would not be present on February 2nd, that he preferred to attend the court hearing. Besides, I said, I had enough of the Selective Service, and if I ever had to have any more dealings with them, it would be too soon.

"Oh, but you have to be present" the clerk said. "You are required to go through the induction process, to the moment of induction. Then you can refuse if you want, but the refusal has to be official." I stared at the receiver in astonishment and rage.

That night I climbed a hill overlooking the town, the frozen Monongahela River arching below, long, empty coal barges lashed to the banks. To the left, a towering university smoke stack mouthed a curly plume as I watched; everywhere snaps of light stared coldly. Of all the times I had come to that spot to ponder, to pray for patience, to pray for strength, this was the neediest.

The ceremony room was empty except for the captain, sergeant, and me, which I really quite liked; it was far more personal, even solemn. It felt like a baptism, which in a way it was, in that it was another measure of my faith. And what again was that faith? Certainly it was a commitment to conscientious objection, that however justified, all wars were evil, evil because they entailed human beings inflicting pain, suffering, and death on others. Most offensive was that this suffering was typically inflicted for ideological reasons. To me, people killing other people was not our right nor our purpose; we should nurture, not destroy life.

In the ceremony, standing eye-to-eye with the captain and the sergeant meant standing eye-to-eye with a moral enemy. The purpose of these men, and that place, was to feed with fresh bodies the killing machine which was the army, and the current killing field which was Vietnam. How baffling it was to me, as the captain again read the ceremonial lines, that these two could perform this function with no apparent qualms. "Duty and tradition," I supposed the sergeant would say; "Laws and regulations," would say the captain.

"Donald Laird Simons, United States Army," snapped the captain, in his best military voice.

"No," I said, in the voice of a human being.

"Donald Laird Simons, United States Army."

"No."

"Donald Laird Simons, United States Army!"

"No!"

As I once again drove from the induction center, I knew it was the last time I would see that place; I should see a prison first. But I was glad, as it turned out, to go through the ceremony again, to refuse again; doing so gave me the strength to continue.

The next day, February 3, 1971, I sat quietly in the courtroom while my attorney and the U.S. Attorney argued, the former reading his motion to nolle the indictment, the government reminding us that a new indictment for my latest refusal would be forthcoming. My lawyer countered with the promise of a new motion to nolle the new indictment. The judge ordered a continuance.

Shortly after this I received a letter from my attorney written in his earlier, ambitious tone:

> Yesterday at Lexington, Kentucky, I heard the attorney for Joe Mulloy tell how he handled his appeal to the Supreme Court of the United States. I think we are likely to do better.

*U.S. v. Mulloy*[27] was an important draft case argued before the Supreme Court on April 20, 1970 and decided in Mulloy's favor. My attorney was interested because of the similarities in our cases; Mulloy's local board did not reopen his classification when he first filed for conscientious objector status, and like me, they denied him that first personal appearance, granting him only a courtesy interview. Admittedly, I was encouraged that Mulloy won in the Supreme Court.

But I once again faced eking out a living for another month or two, until the next court appearance. I chose the physical, but mostly psychological, distance of the Jersey shore, though it remained the off-season. Still I believed I could drum up enough work in the painting trade to get by.

I was wrong. March through May was a disaster; I had virtually no work, despite advertising and putting out handbills. At one point the extent of my savings was a postage stamp.

Over those months, the Philadelphia and New York newspapers helped me keep my mind off my troubles. The big story was the court-martial conviction of Lieutenant William Calley. To both hawk and dove, the case was a symbol for the war

27. *U.S. v. Mulloy*, 398 U.S. 410, 416 (1970).

and the conscience of America, so the conviction aroused massive public reaction.

The verdict was denounced in Congress and state legislatures, resolutions were passed demanding Calley's pardon; several draft boards resigned, mass marches on Washington were planned, and some war veterans gave themselves up to the authorities, claiming they were just as guilty. Several Southern governors, not the least of whom was George Wallace of Alabama, vehemently protested the verdict, and in Indiana the state flag was flown at half staff. Wallace's neighbor, Georgia Governor Jimmy Carter, did not directly attack the verdict, but declared a day in honor of American soldiers, which happened to be the day of Calley's sentencing.

Calley was seen by fellow GIs as "the scapegoat" for higher-ups, some agreeing he was guilty and should be punished, but most siding with combat veterans who termed the verdict "a bum rap." Many felt if Calley was to be punished, so should his superiors. Republican senator from Oregon Mark Hatfield said: "The chain of command leading upward shares in the guilt—so do we all."

As the public clamor rose, President Nixon ordered Calley to be moved from the stockade to his quarters at Fort Benning where he would remain pending a Presidential review. This decision brought a flurry of protests accusing Nixon of "unprecedented intervention"; others defended Nixon's right as Commander-in-Chief of the Armed Forces to review and decide the case.

The Calley affair had the further effect of mobilizing anti-war Vietnam veterans. Members of Vietnam Veterans Against the War (VVAW) staged a massive five-day protest called "Operation Dewey Canyon III" where 700 participants threw their combat medals, ribbons and uniforms onto the Capitol steps.[28]

All the while, other cases of war atrocities surfaced, including the case of Brigadier General John Donaldson, former brigade commander in South Vietnam. Charged with killing six Vietnamese civilians and assaulting two others, the 42 year-old West Point graduate was the highest ranking officer

28. *New York Times*, April 24, 1971, p. 1, 12.

to be accused of killing civilians in the Vietnam War, and the first general to be charged with a war crime since the Philippine insurrection 70 years before. Ultimately, however, the charges against Donaldson were dropped.

In July, after months of stalemate and four years of no progress, the Viet Cong presented a new seven-point peace plan at the Paris talks. They offered to release all American and Allied prisoners of war in North and South Vietnam in return for an American troop pull-out by the end of 1971. But in a subsequent session, Ambassador David K. E. Bruce told the Communists the United States "cannot possibly accept" the proposal as it stood; he conceded, however, that the plan had new elements, and was reason for a "fresh start" in secret negotiations. The Communists though, insisted on open talks.

In September, to halt the Communists' southward push, President Nixon ordered heavy air strikes on fuel depots and other installations in North Vietnam, north of the Demilitarized Zone (DMZ). The DMZ was a five-mile buffer zone running roughly along the seventeenth parallel; it was established in 1954 after the defeat of the French to "temporarily" divide the country while political issues were resolved.

Not long after, South Vietnam's President Nguyen Van Thieu was reelected in a controversial one-man election, garnering 74 percent of the votes cast as 87 percent of the country's eligible voters turned out. The campaign had been marked by protests from students, veterans, and Buddhist groups, who charged the election was rigged. Thieu was sworn in for a second four-year term October 31, with massive security precautions, but the ceremony came off without a hitch as more than 5,000 attended. Representatives from 30 nations were present, including United States Treasury Secretary John B. Connally. To mark the occasion, Thieu freed nearly 3,000 prisoners of war.

The months continued to pass me by with no new court hearings scheduled. Once again it was past Labor Day, so the work which finally came in, petered out. That there had not yet been a trial, an event the U.S. Attorney appeared so anxious for, left me believing he had a change of heart. Once more the optimist in me took over.

# CHAPTER SEVEN
## PEACE ON TRIAL

If I had learned anything from past experience it was to be distrustful of silence from the government. This time proved no exception, as presently a letter came from my attorney advising a trial date had been set for December 13, 1971. I was upset at the news, because I knew this case had no business going to court in the first place. From my perspective the Selective Service had not done its job; "the system" had failed. Of course, the other view was that the Selective Service had done its job very well; by nailing me, they had at least protected the integrity of their system.

Subsequent letters from my attorney had him gearing up for the occasion, as he reviewed his arguments and those lines of reasoning he thought I should fully understand. But his help might as well have been for someone else, as a depression now settled over me.

In his letters he told of how he intended to subpoena all the local board and the State Appeal Board members, that he hoped to have certain others as character witnesses and as experts on the illegality of the war. He described his plan to have my entire Selective Service file read to the jury, following which I would take the stand for a lengthy personal testimony.

I breathed a great sigh. Is that what I wanted? How much simpler to plead guilty and go off to prison for two to five years. But then why should I plead guilty? Guilty of what? Of being loyal to my conscience? Of doing the right thing? Still my lawyer warned me, "The district attorney is likely to say ugly things about you to the jury. . . ."

It was the promise of all the ugliness which had me seriously thinking of leaving the country at that point, so convinced was I of the absurdity of it all. But I was reluctant to accept that exile was all I had left. I was an American citizen entitled to remain and fight it out. It was not as though I were unwilling to serve the country; simply my conscience would not let me serve as a soldier. And did not the law provide for conscientious objection? Should I have to leave the country because a 71-year-old veteran on my local draft board did not believe I was a CO?

Then there was the larger principle. The Constitution said that the United States government was to be "of the people, by the people, and for the people." It seemed to me a citizen should not be forced from the country because of a different point of view, diverse opinions being the very life blood of the country and its history. On principle then, how could I let the government get away with forcing me out?

Even so, I found myself talking with family and friends about exile. In fact, my father looked startled when I said, "I'm looking at the option of leaving the country. You know how ludicrous this has all become. What do you think of my leaving?"

"I'm convinced justice will win out in your case," he said quite plainly, "that you will be vindicated. There's no need to leave the country."

"What do you base that on?" I asked. "Do you know something I don't?"

"Let's just say I trust the American system of justice." He paused. "Besides, we Simonses are fighters."

With this last comment came a remarkable expression on his face; I had never seen it before. Not stern, but appealing, as if saying "if you leave the country I'll be embarrassed and disappointed." All I could do was sit there, speechless and feeling guilty about bringing up the subject.

As for my mother, "Leaving the country is too extreme. I agree with your father that the courts in this country are fair. You'll be all right."

"But would you accept my decision if I decided to leave?"

She looked over at me, then after a pause said, "Reluctantly."

"Why reluctantly?" I said.

"You know what I mean." She would be embarrassed too.

Then there was my older brother. "So if you left the country, you wouldn't be able to come back, would you?"

"No."

"No more getting together once in awhile on a Saturday night?"

"Not unless you want to come to where I am," I said, "although that's apt to be a long way."

He thought a minute, then said, "I'd rather you be there than in prison."

"Not great either way."

"But if you win your case," he said, "that solves the problem, doesn't it?"

"That's a mighty big 'if'."

I also talked to two old high school friends about the war and exile, mainly because we had corresponded during their time in the Marines, including duty in Vietnam. I did not know what I thought they would say, one of them putting it, "What do you expect from a couple of gunners?" I guess I was hoping they would say that yes, from their experience war was evil and futile, and that it should be opposed in every way. But finally their opinion was that I "shouldn't rock the boat." As for leaving the country, on the one hand they thought it was a "cop-out," and on the other, "wise and realistic," given my circumstances.

My friends at the Cafe and newer friends in New Jersey were more sympathetic. In the end though, I asked myself what right I had approaching any of them, even my family, on this matter? If it was permission to leave I was seeking, I was looking in the wrong places. Only I could grant that.

I chose to stay and fight for several reasons. First, I was unwilling to let the government force me from the country. Second, going to trial would add more evidence to the sincerity of my claim. And finally, I was ready to debate the whole issue of war itself, the Vietnam War and all wars, and the fundamental evil of killing in wars. Not going to trial would be to miss this unique opportunity.

# I REFUSE

As I recall, December 13, 1971 was a cold, gray and damp morning. The hour-and-a-half drive to the courthouse in Elkins seemed an eternity to me. At the wheel was a history professor, a Quaker who had written a letter of support for my CO application. Clearly brooding, his eyes were riveted ahead as though going to a religious war. Next to him was my father, frail now from an illness which had him dying by the day. In the back, and next to me, was the professor's Quaker wife. She was an anxious woman; indeed, if her husband was on the way to war, she was already there.

I sat stiffly in a new blue suit and new shoes purchased just for the occasion. Staring out the frosty side window, I searched the depths of the passing leafless forest for a calming image, though my mind continued to return to who we were, where we were going and what we were about to do.

Appreciative and apologetic were my feelings for these people, including my father; I had gotten myself into trouble, and by rights I should get myself out of it. It did not occur to me that they admired me; they wanted to help in whatever way they could.

"You'll be all right," my mother said as we drove away, her face set with a seriousness I had never seen before; she chose to remain at home, believing she would be counter-productive at the trial.

The courthouse reminded me of a post office, possibly because the old post office in Morgantown was also that federal design, pillars in the front, long horizontal concrete steps, metal doors, and gray marble floors. And windows, high divided windows which in the winter looked all the more severe.

The courtroom was on the second floor reached either by a tiny, rickety elevator, or by a narrow marble stairway arching up only as far as the second floor. In fact, that may have been all the floors there were. For me, there were only two floors, or rather only one, the second floor. And only one room.

It was an average-sized courtroom, I supposed, though I had nothing to compare it to. It had bland, institutional beige walls, and heavy, dark furniture; the long, narrow venetian blinds were always closed, no doubt to keep the jurors from daydreaming. A flood of fluorescent light shown overhead, while underfoot was a hard tile floor, worn from years of convictions; it crunched embarrassingly when trod upon by new black shoes.

The trial began with jury selection, my attorney asking me to help from my chair beside him at the long slick, defendant's table. He was presuming, incorrectly, that I knew how to do this. Yet as we went along I got the idea; we needed jurors more apt to be sympathetic to our position. The prosecution struck virtually all the women from the jury; we avoided veterans for their bias, striking all but one; albeit, to our dismay, he became the jury foreman.

The government opened with the commanding officer of the induction center who testified that yes, the young man sitting at the defendant's table twice, in-person, refused induction at his facility. Technically, the trial could have ended right there. Had we said but two words, "no contest," it would have. Instead, our plan was to never quite say yes, the point being that there was much more to this case than one man refusing induction.

At the first opportunity we launched into the issue of conscientious objection, to include reading the jury my entire Selective Service file. The prosecution, however, immediately objected, and was sustained. So much for the Selective Service file. My counsel then offered the draft board's requirements for conscientious objector classification to show how I was entirely qualified for it. The prosecution again objected, and was sustained.

Next we attempted the broader issue of the illegality of the war, the argument being that all induction orders for Vietnam were illegal.

"Objection."

"Sustained."

In frustration, my attorney asked the judge just what he was permitted to argue. The judge said, "only whether Mr. Simons refused induction." With that, everyone looked at each other wondering why we were all still sitting there.

Now, we had built our case based on a provision in the judge's ruling on a pretrial motion:

Accordingly, it is ADJUDGED and ORDERED that the defendant's motion to dismiss the indictment be, and the

same is hereby overruled, with leave granted to raise at a
subsequent time in this criminal proceeding any issue
that defendant may deem appropriate.

My attorney relied on that provision, only to find we were
now denied.

That afternoon my attorney started back at the beginning;
he argued that if we could not read my Selective Service file to
the jury, at least the file should be submitted as evidence; the
jury could read it themselves. That was rejected. We then
sought to present Selective Service rules and regulations generally, to show how dissenters were protected by law. That
went nowhere. Next, my lawyer offered the issue of religion
and moral law, that if the men and women of the jury believed
in God, which they profess to in jury selection, they would
choose the higher law of God over the laws of man, and vote
for acquittal. But it was clear by their expressions, the jurors
had long been prepared to vote otherwise.

In desperation, the defense asked to bring our witnesses
forward, people who had come from as far as Connecticut and
New York. Aware five were university professors, the judge
acquiesced, as did the district attorney, reluctantly.

I was not permitted in the courtroom during this, though I
learned it too was a waste of time. Indeed, for some of our
witnesses it proved an embarrassment, only the most general
of statements were allowed. One professor, a distinguished
expert on Vietnam, had accepted our invitation to the trial
with the promise he would be permitted to argue the illegality of the war. Instead, he was reduced to being a mere character witness, even though he and I had met only briefly on
two occasions.

Then there was my poor father who insisted, despite his ill
health, to be allowed to speak on his son's behalf. But in the
end, he did not have the strength to be heard in the large,
unmicrophoned courtroom.

So ended the first day. As I sat there watching the players
file out, I noted the U.S. Attorney and his assistant closing
their briefcases as if it were any other day at the office; and
for them it was. It then occurred to me that dealing with the
court was like dealing with the Selective Service all over

again. They went strictly by the book; the judge and prosecutor might just as well have been members of my local board. The way things were going, tomorrow night I would be behind bars.

The Quaker professor, his wife, and my father drove back to Morgantown, to return the next morning. At the request of my lawyer, I remained in Elkins, feeling very much under arrest. Our having dinner together at the hotel, he said, was to be a strategy meeting, which proved not to be. Rather it appeared he only wanted to keep an eye on me, lest I do something rash.

I might, for example, go "underground," could in fact go underground right there that very night, albeit he did not know that. My old friend Mac had a cabin on the Middle Fork River near neighboring Buckhannon, where I could hide out. Then, through channels at the Cafe, I could be smuggled out of the state, and even the country. For that matter, with 14 hours before the trial resumed, I could hitch a ride and be half way across the country before dawn.

Meanwhile at dinner, my deep depression and absolute inability to crack a smile so concerned my lawyer that he asked our witnesses from Connecticut and New York to take me out to try to cheer me up; no doubt they too were to keep an eye on me. He confided to one that he feared I might commit suicide, though I never imagined or suggested I could do anything like that.

On the other hand, when later that evening I closed the door to my hotel room, the click of the bolt seemed an invitation to unclick it, to slip down the hall to the fire escape. But did I really think no one would be watching Room 414 through the night? For all I knew the prosecutor was camped out in the hall, laid out in a sleeping bag at my door!

For the first time in my life I felt utterly helpless, like a butterfly in a net. An angry butterfly at that, mostly angry at myself. How could I have been so stupid to think I had a chance of obtaining justice, when from the beginning, from the first induction order I had been denied? The government had me, and they knew it; and now, finally, I knew it too.

My only hope now was to rise above this. I knew that despite my personal defeat, the higher objectives of my resistance had been met; there was no blood on my hands, I had not participated in the military in any capacity. And by so denying the army, and yes, by going to trial, I had touched a lot of people who might not otherwise have seen the war from an anti-war perspective.

"Good morning."

"Good morning."

"Good morning," my attorney, the prosecutor, and I said to each other as we gathered in the lobby with others from the trial. Everyone was so cordial, for a moment I forgot why we were there. Actually, it was the assistant prosecutor greeting us; the district attorney had not expected to go a second day, and was away on other business. Unlike the district attorney, who could pass for a high school track coach, the assistant looked quite sinister, his five o'clock shadow at eight o'clock in the morning making him look ready for the kill. The district attorney returned a short time later, apparently not wanting to miss this.

Entering with my counsel, I spotted my father sitting with the Quaker professor and his wife. Seeing me, he rose as I strode over to him. Oddly, it was as though I had not seen him for years, emotion suddenly gripping my throat. Now it was the fighting Simonses against the government bad guys, against blind justice; I had heard of families pulling together in time of crisis, but this was the first I had felt it. Shaking my father's hand, I could see the pride in his face.

Taking our places around the courtroom for the grand finale, we watched as the bailiff, a nervous, gravelly-voiced, ill-tempered man, barked for all to rise as the judge entered. Unexpectedly though, someone in the middle row of the gallery refused to rise, heads turning to see who it was. Searching too, in a moment I spotted the Quaker professor's wife still seated, in protest. I was elated and wanted to applaud. As such, her statement would be tested, as again the harsh throat of the bailiff issued the order, this time directly at her. Still she did not move. It was as the bailiff looked on the verge of violence, that she slowly rose.

However, it would be down hill from then on, as the by-the-book prosecutors opened by saying they saw no reason to prolong the case, that in their opinion it was ready for the jury.

But the judge noted a couple remaining character witnesses, and otherwise asked the defense if it had anything new. The fact was, all my attorney had was a return to our central themes, his beginning again with conscientious objection. This time though, the judge erupted angrily, threatening counsel with contempt. He then repeated, it was not the purpose of the court to determine whether or not I was a conscientious objector; that was the job of the Selective Service. My attorney responded animatedly that that was the whole point, the Selective Service had not done its job.

The judge leaned back in his big leather chair and proclaimed that all that had been discussed in pretrial hearings; the Selective Service, he said, was not on trial here. All the while, the prosecutors scribbled notes, obviously pleased. Also pleased was the supervisor of the Morgantown draft board, who had slunk in and was smiling broadly from the back of the gallery.

The last of the character witnesses were allowed to say how they knew me, and what sort of person they thought I was, confined strictly to our formal relationship. Thus the jury heard, for example, that I was a responsible person, always on time, and a hard worker, but nothing of the occasions when I expressed my opposition to the war or my reasons for refusing the draft.

That left only closing arguments, or so I thought. To counter any criticism he had not given us every opportunity, the judge called me to the witness stand. I felt the blood drain to my feet. That late in proceedings I was not really prepared, nor I doubted was my lawyer, or even the prosecution, although they did not object. Thus, with new black shoes crunching on the hard tile floor, I crossed the room to the witness chair, well aware every eye in the place was on me. Yet as I crossed, suddenly it occurred to me that this might be our big break. Such was in the cautious gaze of my lawyer as I turned and sat down. Indeed with my swearing in, he went right to the heart of it. "Would you like to tell the court just why you refused military induction?"

Strange the thoughts which come under pressure. I had not read Thoreau's "On the Duty of Civil Disobedience" for two years, but suddenly to mind came the line, "What I have to do

121

is to see, at any rate, that I do not lend myself to the wrong which I condemn."[29] But I decided that quoting it would not make much sense, not without an explanation. Instead, I chose a more general statement "I do not want to lend myself to the destruction of other human beings."

Even so, no sooner had I said this than a look of great anxiety crossed my lawyer's face, the prosecutors looking up, and the judge leaning forward.

"Thank you, Mr. Simons," the judge said quickly. "You may step down."

If the jurors and the people in the gallery were puzzled, no less so was I. It was only after getting back to my chair that I realized what had happened. The next logical question would have been to explain why I was unwilling to so lend myself, to which I would have responded, "Because I am a conscientious objector." The appearance would be that we had maneuvered back to the issue of conscientious objection in defiance of the judge's warning; doing so would have brought a contempt charge.

The judge made one more feeble attempt to make the trial appear fairer than it was. At the last minute he offered to allow my Selective Service file to be taken by the jury into their deliberations. But my attorney objected as there was no

---

29. Henry David Thoreau, *Walden, and "On the Duty of Civil Disobedience"* (New York: New American Library, 1960), pp. 228–229.

Unjust laws exist: shall we be content to obey them, or shall we endeavor to amend them, and obey them until we have succeeded, or shall we transgress them at once? Men generally, under such a government as this, think that they ought to wait until they have persuaded the majority to alter them. They think that, if they should resist, the remedy would be worse than the evil . . .

If the injustice is part of the necessary friction of the machine of government, let it go, let it go: perchance it will wear smooth,—certainly the machine will wear out. If the injustice has a spring, or a pulley, or a rope, or a crank, exclusively for itself, then perhaps you may consider whether the remedy will not be worse than the evil; but if it is of such a nature that it requires you to be the agent of injustice to another, then, I say, break the law. Let your life be a counter friction to stop the machine. What I have to do is to see, at any rate, that I do not lend myself to the wrong which I condemn.

way of knowing they would read it. The judge sustained the objection, and the file was not with the jurors when they retired.

In a way, I felt sorry for the jurors. They had to sit through a trial which was essentially over in the first 20 minutes. The judge had permitted no defense; the only evidence they had to rule on was the testimony of the commanding officer from the induction center. So, following a brief deliberation, the jury handed down the only verdict they could, "guilty as charged." But if that stung, it would sting 12 more times with the poll of the jury, my eyes passing from member to member as each condemned me to my face.

I expected to be behind bars in the judge's next breath, and for the ensuing two to five years. Indeed, that would have been the result had he not suddenly gotten the Christmas spirit. Astonishingly, he permitted me to remain free on the existing $1,000 property bond, until the sentencing date in January; "So you can be with your family for the holidays," he said.

"We cannot guarantee Mr. Simons' freedom beyond January," the district attorney warned, obviously angered by the judge's decision.

But there it ended, leaving me to wonder if it had not been divine intervention which still had me a free man. Later I learned it was not uncommon for defendants with clean records to be allowed freedom prior to sentencing to settle their affairs; but I preferred to think it divine intervention.

Back in the car the Quaker professor and his wife called the trial a Nazi kangaroo court; my father, meanwhile, sat in stunned silence. For my part, I was numb and disoriented, as from a nightmare.

Statistics from the years 1967 to 1975 put my conviction in perspective. Unlike the years prior to the Vietnam conflict when conviction was almost inevitable in draft cases, between 1967 and 1975 the percentage of unsuccessful defendants decreased every year. For example, in 1967, 75 percent were convicted, as opposed to just over 36 percent by 1970. Then by 1975, less than 17 percent of all draft law defendants were convicted.

In 1967, nearly 90 percent of those convicted went to prison, the percentage dropped to half that in 1970; by 1975, less than

9 percent served time. Over time, the average length of sentences likewise dropped. For instance, in 1968 the average was 37.3 months, as opposed to 14.5 months in 1974.[30] Further, when I was convicted on December 14, 1971, only 33 percent of all draft cases nationally resulted in conviction; thus, I estimated the federal court handling my case was probably five years behind the times. How conservative it really was, would be apparent on sentencing day.

Prison? How would it be? *The Handbook for Conscientious Objectors*, published by the Central Committee for Conscientious Objectors, offered some idea.[31] To begin with, prison authorities viewed draft violators as square pegs in round holes. As a group they were more intelligent, more independent, and less easily deterred by fear than the conventional convict. Also, unlike the usual prisoner, many COs had small but vocal support groups watching over them from the outside.

Though treatment in prison tended to vary widely, in general COs got a better break than the average convict. Historically, because of their intelligence and ability, they took over many of the clerical and "soft" jobs. Also, where convicts prone to defiance were often ruthlessly suppressed, these days rebellious COs were, more often than not, treated by "administrative segregation."

Conscientious objectors got a varying and often conflicting reception from other inmates. The exuberance of some COs was the source of a fair amount of friction, especially in those prisons where inmates were serving long terms. Ironically, many inmates had a flag-waving patriotism which conflicted with that expressed by the dissenters. Many regarded a man who went to prison purely for his beliefs as a "sucker." Also, many inmates, particularly those who had already done considerable time and were thoroughly indoctrinated with prison totalitarianism, frowned on the behavior of some COs who challenged prison rules and regulations. These inmates feared

30. Kohn, p. 89.
31. Arlo Tatum, ed., *Handbook for Conscientious Objectors* (10th ed.; Central Committee for Conscientious Objectors; Philadelphia: Larchwood Press, 1968), pp. 71–83.

the COs would get them all in trouble, as during World War II with CO action to achieve racial equality in prison. During that war, Danbury Federal Prison saw a work strike over the policy of racial segregation in the dining hall. Protesting this policy, 19 COs were confined to their cells with reduced exercise and visiting privileges. After 135 days which saw mounting support both inside and outside the prison, the policy was finally changed.[32]

Generally, most COs found they were socially accepted, for though prison society was sharply stratified, it was much more closely bound together than any outside community of such widely varied components. The inmates all had the same problem, including a dislike of those who stood between them and freedom. Furthermore, COs who stood up against the force of prison officialdom typically gained a certain respect from the other prisoners, and COs in punishment often received sub-rosa help from other inmates.

I imagined my first stop after sentencing would be a local or county jail controlled by a sheriff and staffed by spoils system appointees. I heard that the personnel in these jails were typically more brutal and conditions worse than in the federal prison system. Up to two-fifths of a county jail population consisted of men convicted of no crime, but merely awaiting trial. Others, like myself, would be waiting for transportation to a federal institution.

Living conditions and regulations at the local and county jails varied widely. But generally, housing was in crowded cells furnished only with bunk beds (poor or no springs, often no mattresses), dirty blankets (sheets very rare), a toilet, wash basin, and perhaps a box or table. These cells were often filthy and shared with many-legged occupants. Food may or may not be adequate. The diet otherwise was monotonous, unbalanced, and of low quality. On the other hand, in many jails the diet could be supplemented with commissary purchases such as candy, fruit, and even whole meals, but commissary prices

32. Robert Cooney and Helen Michalowski, eds., *The Power of the People: Active Nonviolence in the United States* (Philadelphia: New Society Publishers, 1987), p. 107.

were often exorbitant. Conditions in the smaller towns were said to be better than in those of large cities.

I assumed my correspondence would be censored, but there would probably be no restrictions on the number of letters I could send or receive. Visiting conditions in the jails, however, were frequently atrocious. It was often reduced to yelling above jailhouse bedlam through screens so heavy the visitor could scarcely be seen. Some jails permitted daily visits by any number of persons, while others restricted them. Ministers and lawyers, by contrast, could usually see a prisoner under more decent conditions.

Daily life in county jail was a combination of sleep, food, talk, noise, reading, and idleness. There was typically no work program, no yard or recreation facilities and inadequate lighting for reading. In some jails inmates were locked up in cells nearly all the time. In other places, they were locked out of their cells and kept in a long, bare room called the tank.

The Department of Justice would determine the federal prison where I would be sent. Upon receipt of orders, a U.S. marshal, at a time convenient to him, would transfer me. The duration of my stay in a county jail would vary from a few days to a several weeks. Transferring could be done individually or when the marshall had several prisoners to take at once.

With all this in mind, I asked myself what would be gained by going to prison? If I was interested in being a martyr for the peace movement, then prison was one way to do it. It might also be the solution if I was concerned about my "honor." But in the end, I came to the conclusion that I was simply one man, responding to the call of his conscience. Sure, I was part of a movement of people opposed to war, but I did not have to do what society or the peace movement considered honorable or appropriate. I had gone to trial to complete my statement of opposition to violence and war. Had not that goal been achieved?

Some would argue that only by going to prison would my statement be complete. I thought about that. But my case did not have the national prominence of a David Harris, an early noncooperator who turned in his draft card and served a prison term. When I was behind bars and out of sight, I would be out of mind. So what more was to be gained? I must add that David Harris and other prominent members of the resistance were enormously inspiring. They were in the same league with Martin Luther King, a cut above the rest of us; true heroes of the era, they inspired a generation to resistance— including me.

Each of us did what he could in his way. We could not all react like Martin Luther King, or hope to be as effective as those who had high visibility and access to the media. The statements and impact of the rest of us were destined to be on a far smaller scale, determined by individual circumstance, personality, and spirit.

Three days after the trial I drove my parents and grand-mother to the airport where they boarded a plane to begin their Christmas vacation. As I hugged my mother and grand-mother, and shook my father's hand, their faces seemed a picture in contrast. My grandmother, who had just joined us, did not understand my problems, probably by choice, her face now oblivious to all but the roar of the airplane engines be-hind. Worry tightened my mother's face, although she nodded acceptingly with our hug. My father was also aware of my plans, his look of disillusionment from the trial replaced again by pride in me. It would be the last I saw him or my grand-mother alive, illness taking both within six months.

Back home I exchanged my parent's car for my brother's small pick-up truck, which he let me borrow for this occa-sion. However, trouble starting it in the falling temperatures had me on edge once again. Meanwhile, my attention was drawn repeatedly to the window at my shoulder, framing as it did the family homestead just visible through the ice; I wondered whether I would ever see it again. Just then the engine started.

No time to delay. Finding first gear, I eased out the clutch. The little truck crept stiffly from the narrow parking spot; the frozen tires thumped from being in one shape so long. Then, with a final look to the house, I was away.

Two blocks down was Third Street where I shifted gears for the long descent to Beechurst Avenue. Along the way I passed street corners where, in grade school, I stood as captain of the safety patrol, decked out as I was in my heavy yellow rain coat, spotless patrol belt across the shoulder and around the waist, and on top a handsome pith helmet. I looked like a little soldier.

Beechurst Avenue was the site of such familiar landmarks as Chico's Dairy, Tony's Restaurant, Freddie's Tavern, and Mutt's Place, a tavern catering to the workers of the Seneca Glass factory. They were neighborhood scenes I had grown up with; I watched them flash past this last time.

Out through Evansdale Campus, I peered up at the gray brick Engineering Building I visited so often with my father. Below it, the circular Creative Arts Center where I did my graduate work. From here on, only a memory.

Familiar too was the Interstate to Pittsburgh, my accelerating into the all but empty highway; in a few more days, many West Virginians would be driving to visit family and friends for the holidays. Not me. Nor as I neared Pittsburgh would I be stopping to see my draft counselor, or any "good doctors." Strange how all that seemed so long ago. As I passed Pittsburgh though, and the road became unfamiliar, my anxiety markedly rose; the reality of what I was doing sunk in.

Then, almost to Erie, Pennsylvania, a snow squall came out of nowhere. The Interstate froze instantly, spinning the lightweight truck out of control. I banged along backwards down the guardrail at 65 miles an hour. A desperate shifting to progressively lower gears was to no avail, the tires were simply spinning in place. In another moment it did not matter, the guardrail ended and I went careening, still backwards, over an embankment. Snow flying, I landed at the edge of some trees, miraculously still right side up.

But now the truck's four-cylinder motor, perhaps in shock, would not start again, as if it could pull me up the frozen embankment anyway. Climbing from the cab, I looked to the highway above.

In a steady downpour of snow, my duffel bag over my shoulder, I struggled to the road side, there to stick out my thumb to the nearly empty highway. As the blinding snow steadily accumulated on my hatless head, I thought "what a fitting end." I would be found frozen to death on the side of the road, destination unknown. How the motorist who finally stopped happened to see me I never knew. Nor was he to know my secret.

I spent the night in a midtown Erie hotel, then early the next morning rode with a tow truck back out to the Interstate. As it turned out, the night's rest had apparently been good for the little truck, as it started right up; a hoist back to the highway had me again loading my duffel.

During what proved a sunny few hours, I soon passed into New York State where I traveled the thruway along massive Lake Erie, visible to my left. On reaching the southern beltway around Buffalo, however, it began to cloud up again.

Without hesitation, I drove onto the Peace Bridge, an ironic name I thought given the circumstances. Peace had been at the heart of my effort from the beginning; now it was the name of a bridge taking me into exile.

But my thoughts did not end there. To mind again, my father's parting words, "You now have my full support to leave the country, son." He added, "No matter what happens to me, you stay where you are, you take care of yourself."

I wondered how many young Americans preceded me, and how many would follow? To what extent were their experiences and emotions the same and different? I could not know, except that in crossing that bridge, I felt like I was the only one who had ever done it. There was a certain euphoria in the knowledge I was denying those who would have me behind bars, but it was mixed with feelings of sadness. I knew Americans to be well-meaning and generous people, except where they were deluded into a destructive point of view; it was this same point of view which now had me an enemy. Was this not further evidence of the evil of war?

# CHAPTER EIGHT
## AFTERLIFE

Stopped at the Canadian customs booth at the far end of the Peace Bridge, the officer asked my purpose for coming to Canada. I was not about to say "political asylum," or "exile"; I did not want to jeopardize my chances. I had read enough about this act to know I must get into the country first. So I said, "visiting, just visiting." Judging by my age and grim expression, however, I doubt he completely believed I was *just* visiting.

For all I knew he would ask me right there whether I was coming to Canada because of the American draft, whether I was in fact a "draft dodger," as war resisters were called in Canada. Had I been asked, I would have said, "No," because I was something other than that, although I was not quite sure what. In *Guide to the Draft*, the authors spoke of the "unsuccessful cooperator," which I supposed I was; then again, I was also a convicted felon. Certainly, I would not volunteer that.

As it turned out I was not asked, and for a very specific reason. A recent Canadian government ruling forbade border and immigration officials from asking Americans about their draft status, the government deciding it was irrelevant for visiting or immigration. As it was, the man in the booth only asked a few routine customs questions, then wished me a pleasant visit.

My destination was Toronto, one of the major centers for American draft resisters; I knew I could get assistance there. Before I left Morgantown a Methodist campus minister, who had supported my CO claim, gave me the phone number of an exile he met during an ecumenical tour of Canada. I was to contact Tony and his wife Judy as soon as I got there.

It was amazing how tightly I held the piece of paper with that name and phone number; it was one of few threads holding me together just then. Since leaving my hometown the day before, I had seen little that was familiar, and certainly no faces that I knew. I had scarcely spoken to anyone. And here I was in a foreign country, bouncing along a parkway into a city I knew nothing about, and in which I knew no one, except for those on that piece of paper.

I decided to spend the night in a small motel on the outskirts of town until I got oriented. It was gray and snowing heavily as I peered out the curtains toward Lake Ontario, a scenic spot during the summer I was sure, but dark and lonely that evening. As I watched, the motel sign creaked back and forth in the stiff wind; there was barely a sign of life on the road out front.

Later that evening I called my attorney, since we had not spoken since the trial. For the moment, he seemed relieved when I told him where I was. On the other hand, it was not a long conversation, apparently intentionally on his part, as within a week a message came warning me of wire taps; I was to be careful not to create more trouble for myself. Unsigned, the card bore a postmark from a town in Pennsylvania, where I recalled my attorney had a relative.

At first I did not take this clandestine message seriously; it seemed a bit paranoid. What could I say over the phone that would get me into trouble? But he was right, there was no telling what might happen if the FBI learned of my intention to stay in Canada. I decided I would heed the warning.

Next I called my family to let them know I was safe. My brother sounded very relieved, an uncharacteristic crack of emotion in his voice. He could just as easily have been against me, but proved instead to be one of my strongest defenders. I often wondered what he would have done if he had been ordered to report for induction. But, it was not an issue between us; it was enough to know that he supported me.

I also had great feelings of solidarity with my father, because he continued to stand by me when many fathers would have, and did, disown their sons. The solidarity I felt with my mother, however, was different; while she supported me, as my mother, I had the feeling she would rather I had gone into the army. How could I forget her earlier references to her brother who served during World War II? Was not this the measure she held me to, as indeed did that brother and his family? They would never understand, I was sure, and now even less.

But on that snowy night of December 18, 1971 it did not matter who approved or disapproved, who understood or did not; it was enough that I accepted what I had done.

The first thing the next morning I opened the piece of paper with the name and phone number, and called Tony. I did not know whether the campus minister had contacted him, or if he was expecting to hear from me, but he sounded glad to hear my voice. When I told him I was in a motel on Lakeshore Boulevard near Exhibition Place, he gave me directions.

Tony and Judy's apartment was over a small store in an uptown area four miles from the motel. When I met them I was surprised by how they looked; I suppose I was expecting a more counterculture look, perhaps long hair, "love beads," and sandals. I quickly learned that appearance was an important matter in Canada, that to become a landed immigrant and be under the protection of the Canadian government, it was advantageous to look conservative.

Passing the morning with Tony, a student from Buffalo, and his Canadian wife, I learned more about immigration. For instance, I had to file for landed status soon. When I did, I had to highlight my most positive qualities and be prepared to convince them that they should let me in.

Suddenly I became anxious. Wasn't I already in? Tony assured me they would do all they could, but there were no guarantees. One thing was certain though, I was welcome to stay at their place during the attempt. Then, as a further gesture of their hospitality, they gave me a "tuque," a heavy knit cap. "Welcome to Canada," they said. The tuque was my constant companion those first days, especially as Tony and Judy soon departed for Christmas in Montreal.

In the sparse, but appealing one-bedroom flat, the large front room and its couch became my headquarters. I often simply gazed out the front window in disbelief of where I was.

From the second floor I had a good view of the narrow, busy, uptown street, electric buses humming and clacking by every 20 minutes. Electric buses? They did not have those in Morgantown.

Directly across was an old apartment building, actually a three-story brick house converted into apartments, typical of the older areas of the city. Next to it across a side street, was a one-story eatery, Latvian owned; apparently, many Toronto restaurants were owned and operated by ethnic immigrants. I had breakfast at this one often.

A photographer's studio was next door, where I would have a passport photo taken. Across the street was a drab lunch-dinner restaurant and bar, where I sought a friendly face a few times during the lonely holidays.

"Are you a Yank?" one fellow asked over a third round of beers, as we watched a hockey game at the crowded bar. Was it so obvious that I did not have a clue what I was watching? Just because hockey was the Canadian national sport. . . . "I'm visiting some friends," I said, feeling paranoid, afraid to talk except in the most general terms.

Back toward the apartment was a noisy, oily service station that featured a "government licensed mechanic," something else I had never heard of. An equally noisy and greasy hamburger joint was adjacent to it, followed by a government liquor store called an LCBO, which stood for Liquor Control Board of Ontario. Meanwhile, to get beer, one had to go to a separate store a few blocks away called "Brewer's Retail." Then there was the neighborhood store directly below the apartment, one of those places that had everything and nothing you needed. I found all this odd, yet fascinating.

The most impressive sight from the windows of the apartment was a castle on the hill out back. Later I learned it was called Casa Loma, a privately built and owned structure now open to the public, and a landmark to Torontonians.

Still, my fascination with all this was short-lived as the emotions of my circumstances surfaced. I made these journal entries.

12/21/71: I feel a tremendous insecurity which is not easy to overcome. I am trying hard to counter the anxiety. It must be surmounted. Canada is a beautiful country, Toronto an excellent city. There are many positive things here.

12/22/71: The problem remains this insecurity. No home. Knowing next to no one. The emotion is of losing one's way. Only there is no going home. No returning to familiarity. My task now is to force a new familiarity. I must assimilate what I can, as much as I can, but not too quickly, though time is of the essence.

Christmas Eve 1971: Sitting here alone, do I ever expect to see the United States again? Never.

On Christmas Day I called my parents and told them of the gift of the tuque. They said they could not picture me in a hat, that they did not think I liked hats. I said I did now. It seemed like a phone call across town, the words "I'll stop over later" creeping to my lips. Finally I simply said, "Merry Christmas and, well, thank you." They had not abandoned me. But as the phone quietly hung up on other side, "across town" felt a million miles away.

On Tony and Judy's return I went back to dealing with the immigration business. Tony introduced me to another exile who explained that in my application for landed-immigrant status it was desirable to show financial stability, and a job offer in Canada. He offered to help. As a bank manager, he would provide several thousand dollars to be used just for immigration, while his wife, a psychologist in private practice, would contribute a simulated job offer. Regarding the latter, the idea was to have a prospective job as suited to one's qualifications as possible. Because I had a degree in Psychology, and a Masters Degree in Drama, I was to be offered the position of "Assistant in Psychodrama."

He told me I would have to have documents sent up from the States, including my birth certificate, high school diploma and college transcripts. He recommended that I provide letters from adults of good standing in my former community attesting to my stability and good moral character. I also needed proof of previous employment, bank statements, vehicle ownership, and so on. I knew that getting all this would take time; and time now became very precious, for my sentencing date was set for January 28th. I had to be under the protection of the Canadian government by then.

Meanwhile, my parents sent me a series of letters from my attorney. Initially, I was reluctant to open them, because I considered all that past history. In the end though, I got out the letter opener.

In his correspondence of January 20, he reminded me of the sentencing date, now but a week away, saying I should "be governed accordingly." "I will attend and argue your right to have the verdict set aside, which I believe the present state of the record requires." He went on to say, "I have done a substantial amount of research . . . and it seems inconceivable to me that the present verdict will be allowed to stand. I still have considerable confidence the judge will do the right thing."

But my attorney knew I was in Canada, hence the attached handwritten note: "If you fail to be present at the hearing, your bond will be forfeited, and if you are apprehended, a much higher bond with sureties will be demanded, or you may be denied bond. A larger sentence will be imposed if you should be convicted on retrial."

In another letter he recapped his strategy in our case, noting in what ways we had been denied justice. He went on to provide copies of three motions he had submitted to the court to have the verdict set aside.

By now, however, I was being counseled by the Toronto Anti-Draft Programme (TADP) on the various ways to immigrate. Their literature described them:

> The Toronto Anti-Draft Programme is the largest group in Canada helping young American immigrants who refuse to fight against Vietnam. This Programme provides legal research and information to the other Canadian aid groups and is in contact with some 2,000 draft counsellors in the U.S., providing background information, reporting changes in immigration practice, and verifying or denying the ever-present rumors [regarding U.S. indictments, threats of extradition, amnesty, etc.].

Full-time trained counsellors are available to advise people planning to immigrate; the Programme also helps immigrants once they arrive in Canada. Nearly 200 Torontonians have offered to house new arrivals temporarily. Our Employment Service has a full-time counsellor to help find job offers for applicants and job leads for landed immigrants. Several Toronto lawyers advise immigrants who have special legal problems, and a number of physicians help with medical problems.

The Programme is assisted by dozens of volunteers, both new immigrants and Canadians. Church groups and faculty members from the University of Toronto and York University have been especially valuable sources of assistance and support.

Now though, it was January 28. I could picture the courtroom back in West Virginia, and what must be happening in my absence. A subsequent letter from my attorney described the scene. He said he tried several explanations of why I was not there, and need not have been. But the district attorney did not buy this and demanded to know where I was, to which my lawyer responded, he did not know. The district attorney then accused him of "not cooperating in their effort to apprehend" me, to which my lawyer replied that he thought he was entitled to know where he himself stood legally, that he was at the moment merely being noncommittal.

As a result the judge forfeited my personal recognizance, and issued a bench warrant for my arrest. Meanwhile in Toronto, I was just receiving the last of my personal documents. I was told that one other document, while not absolutely required, would be helpful: a U.S. passport. Apparently, it would give me that much more credibility and support with Immigration. On the other hand, at that late date I was concerned the United States embassy in Toronto might have some record of me. I did not want to repeat an incident where an exile was arrested at the embassy and transported back to the States. Still it was imperative that I get landed status, so I decided to give it a try.

137

When the day came to pick up the passport, I walked through the heavy front doors of the consulate on University Avenue. Though apprehensive, I was determined not to give myself away. Stepping in line at a long counter in a room looking much like a bank, I was struck by how slow the transactions were occurring, or so it seemed to me. As in a bank, I wondered whether there were surveillance cameras, albeit I would not rouse suspicion by looking for them. Then as luck would have it, just as it was my turn, the clerk closed her station; I had to get in another line. All the while I had visions of a repeat of my original arrest, two men stepping up, serving me a warrant, and taking me out to a waiting car.

While waiting in line I wondered about the legality of being arrested at an embassy. Being in the consulate was, of course, the same as being on United States soil, but what about the car? A car was not an embassy. Was being in a U.S. government vehicle the same as being on American soil? Obviously, I would have to be led out across the Canadian sidewalk; what was the law there? It smacked too much of kidnapping to me, and yet there were reported instances of it. These thoughts did little to ease my anxiety.

Just then I was at the counter, where I cleared my voice and leaned forward with my name. Did my self-consciousness give me away? Surely she noted I was of draft age; would she alert security? Consequently, it seemed an eternity as she went to a line of tables with rows of boxes containing passports; I could only hope they were in alphabetical order. All the while, I looked steadily ahead, trying to appear as though this was something I did all the time. Her returning with the document came as a great relief, as did walking out the front door.

As it turned out, this experience was good training for what happened next. The Toronto Anti-Draft Programme convinced me that it would be advantageous to apply for landed-immigrant status at the border, rather than from within Canada. The third option was applying from within the United States which, for me, was now out of the question.

Filing at the border was the quickest way to get landed status, and had several other advantages; first, a decision was made on the spot. In addition, if I was denied, I would be permitted to withdraw the application, meaning I could reapply. Also, a job offer would count for evaluation points at the border, but not if I applied from within Canada. And finally, at the border I would be dealing with less Americanized officers than those who worked at the consulates; so, there was less risk of being rejected.

The Toronto Anti-Draft Programme also continually updated information on border points that were the most favorable, and on shifts where immigration officers were known to be more receptive to young Americans.

So it was that a week after failing to appear in court for sentencing, I put on a suit and tie, grabbed all my forms and documents, and called TADP. They told me I should cross back into the States at the Peace Bridge, and drive up the American side. Passing the Niagara Falls Bridge, I was to return to Canada at Queenston. Officers at the border crossings were in contact with each other, which was the reason for skipping Niagara Falls; it would be suspicious if by some chance I was noted at the Peace Bridge only to be spotted immediately recrossing at Niagara Falls. I was told that seven o'clock that evening was the best time to arrive at Queenston.

But here was the rub. United States customs officers had print-outs from the Justice Department of fugitives who were at-large. When crossing from Canada back into the States, I would have to stop and answer questions from one of these customs officers. What if, because of my draft age, he asked to see identification. Spotting my name on his list, I could be arrested on the spot; there would be nothing the Canadian government could do to help me. It was a risk I had to be prepared to take.

Climbing back into my brother's pick-up truck I headed out of the city. That itself was unnerving as Toronto had given me a sense of security over the past weeks. Anxiously, I turned south on Queen Elizabeth Way, attempting to boost my confidence by glancing across the center median and imagining a jubilantly landed Don Simons bounding back up the other side. On the other hand, I could just as easily imagine him being arrested at the border, and returned to a county jail in West Virginia.

Past Burlington, the ever-present Lake Ontario suddenly opened to Hamilton Harbor, just as the Queen Elizabeth Way became a bridge high overhead; beyond it the industrial city of Hamilton. Further south stretched some flat lands, stitched with scraggly grape vines, the extent of Ontario's wine industry. Approaching St. Catherines I knew the border was 30 minutes away; the Peace Bridge, however, was farther to the south. Meanwhile I glanced to Highway 405 as I passed, the highway from which I would emerge if successful.

Time passed quickly and soon I spotted Fort Erie, Ontario, a small town built low on the western bank of the Niagara River; imposing Buffalo was on the opposite shore. When I descended the hill to the river I pulled to the side of the road, stopped and took a deep breath. "Slow down," I told myself, my heart pumping with anticipation.

Peering out to my left, I observed a fluttering line of Canadian flags, red and white with the broad maple leaf raised as though in an open-palmed gesture of peace. In the distance was a stand of American flags, striped imperially and on guard. How odd this reversal—the previous month I was apprehensive about Canada and the unknown it represented, now it was the other way around. I did not know what awaited me on the American side of that bridge, now but minutes away; would my efforts of the past weeks possibly be all for naught? Certainly it was a gamble; however, I was willing to bet, bureaucracy being what it was, that the fugitive lists at the border did not yet contain my name.

Still as I eased the truck back into gear, I was reminded of the tragedy of it all. I was afraid of my own country. Where once there was trust, now there was only paranoia, to the extent that I felt like I was trying to cross the Berlin Wall.

The Niagara River was quite wide at Fort Erie, a strong winter wind scuffing the surface white; the bridge was high enough to see for miles in both directions. Presently it descended, the line of cars picking up speed, only to come to an abrupt halt at a row of U.S. customs booths. Rolling down my window, I tried to appear calm.

"Citizenship?" asked the customs officer.

"American," I said carefully.

"Destination?"

140

"Morgantown, West Virginia," my following a little too defensively with, "I've been on vacation."

Glancing to the side of him, I noticed a list of names on a clipboard by his wall phone. Was it the Justice Department list, or merely frequently dialed numbers? No, they were names, not numbers. I looked up to see him studying me. I imagined him wondering, if I had been on vacation, why was there no luggage in the truck, and why was I so dressed up? Then there was my age. There were no government restrictions on this side forbidding close questioning, and I was worried he would pull me aside.

Just then he looked up at the overhead lights, revealing as they did the increasing snow fall, the hot exhaust from the growing line of cars behind me spiralling impatiently. Glancing at his watch, he retrieved a timetable from his vest pocket on which possibly were listed shift changes, or maybe scheduled meal or coffee breaks. Then again, it might not be a timetable at all, my eyes growing wide with anxiety. After another moment, however, he looked over at me as though surprised I was still there, his expression my signal to move on. Gingerly then, I accelerated away.

Still there was the long drive up the American side to the Queenston crossing, with a plethora of other worries. For example, was the customs officer suspicious enough to alert the other border crossings, or possibly the state police? What if the car broke down and the police stopped to see if I needed assistance? A routine check of the license number on their computer network would reveal I was not the truck's owner, an investigation of my identification divulging my fugitive status. What if I made a wrong turn and got lost? I would miss the critical 7:00 p.m. crossing time. As it was, I would be lucky to make it because I had apparently miscalculated the distance. I could make up some time with the accelerator, but I dare not get stopped for speeding.

Driving up Interstate 190, I suddenly felt exhilarated as feelings of danger and anticipation combined. I was risking it all for the promise of freedom when I crossed again into Canada. Thinking ahead to Queenston, I savored how different it would be this time; for one, I would not be telling the Canadian officer I was only visiting. Yet, I worried how they would treat me there, fretting now that TADP had sent me to the wrong crossing for that day, or the right crossing but the wrong time.

Just then though, the unexpected: ahead was a toll booth at South Grand Island Bridge, and me with a cashier's check for $3,200, but no cash. In an effort to remember all the other things I had to bring with me, I put no dollars or coins in my pocket.

But that was not all. As I sat there in a string of five cars inching toward the hopper, I saw I was in the wrong line; I needed to be two lines over, where I could speak to an attendant. Then as luck would have it, there was a New York State trooper just beyond the booth, poised to catch cheaters. I looked at my watch, slumping as the cars continued to inch forward.

That was when it occurred to me. At the beginning of December I had driven that same truck from New Jersey back to West Virginia, toll booths all along the Pennsylvania Turnpike. Usually, when I made that trip I put change in the glove compartment of whatever car I drove. With that thought I had everything out of the glove compartment—maps, screwdrivers, a pair of pliers, a bottle opener—and yes, finally a handful of coins accumulated during who knows how many trips to where. I breathed a great sigh as I pulled up to the hopper.

I had to be careful to avoid two branching highways at the North Grand Island Bridge; Moses Parkway and Pine Avenue both led to Niagara Falls. As instructed, I was to bypass that border point to avoid arousing suspicion. As I slipped into the center lane, I watched the exit signs flash past.

But now it was 7:00 p.m. and I still had 10 miles to go; I hoped that the immigration shift I needed was just beginning rather than finishing. Possibly it was in the middle of a four to midnight rotation, but I had no way of knowing. As I continued along though, the Queenston lights in the distance lifted my spirits.

At precisely 7:10, I pulled into the Canadian customs booth where I did exactly as TADP instructed. When the officer asked me the routine tourist-oriented question, I said I wanted to apply for landed-immigrant status. Then, as I was told he would say, the officer directed me to the customs house. The inside was shades of gray metal and concrete with fluorescent lights, a typical government building. Inside, one still felt cold and damp, perhaps due to the proximity of the Niagara River. As it turned out, the man who directed me to the building was not the one to interview me, nor was I interviewed by another at the long, front metal counter. In fact, it was only after the second man disappeared and then returned that I learned a third officer would be with me momentarily.

Presently, a short, middle-aged man with a slight limp approached. He led the way, giving his name and pointing to an office down the hall; meanwhile, I tried to relax.

The lack of decoration in the office suggested it was more of an interview room than his office. He began, "I believe you have some papers for me." Eagerly, I handed him my folder. That he scarcely looked at me seemed odd, but not unusual, according to what I read in preparation; typically, these interviews were not very formal.

As I wondered whether he would ask me about my draft status, I again reminded myself that border officials were instructed that an applicant's draft status was not relevant when applying to enter Canada; indeed, according to the *Manual For Draft-Age Immigrants to Canada*, most did not ask.[33] However, some immigration officers were not beyond getting this information indirectly, by subtle questioning. I was prepared for this, and otherwise well aware that everything I said and did would affect what was written in the "Officer's Personal Assessment."

Mainly, I was not to pretend I had never heard of the Selective Service. The officers assumed young Americans crossing were potential draft offenders; any kind of coyness was apt to irritate them and make them suspicious of one's integrity and honesty. I was to be frank, short on political and ethical sermons, to the point of admitting I might not have considered emigrating were it not for the draft. Nonetheless, I would emphasize that my final decision was based on

---

33. Byron Wall, ed., *Handbook for Draft-Age Immigrants to Canada* (5th ed.; Toronto: House of Anansi, 1970).

an appreciation of Canada, and a determination to become a good citizen.

Still, the detached expression on this immigration officer's face suggested that he was disinclined to challenge me. He seemed to fit the profile of a typical immigration official that I had come to expect. I imagined him to be a family man who liked fishing, and went to church on Sunday. Clean-shaven with a crew cut and a slight paunch, he seemed the picture of contentment, a peace he appeared unwilling to abandon on my account.

Even so, I was nervous about my job offer, custom-made as it was for that moment. It was perfectly within his authority to question it closely, to quiz me on how I had obtained it, and what the job would involve; he might very well phone the employer. But happily, no such scrutiny came. Maybe it was the convincing look of the letterhead the psychologist had handcrafted for the occasion.

Things were going so smoothly that I wondered if I was going to be turned over to a chief immigration officer for more detailed questioning. I was convinced that was next, as my interviewer excused himself and took my papers across the hall.

But he soon returned; if there was a chief immigration officer across that hall, he only contributed his signature to my paperwork. The next thing I knew I was back down at the long metal counter, filling out a customs form declaring the truck and my personal possessions. He gave me a copy of this form along with a "Canadian Immigrant's Record Card." I was to present the latter to my employer as proof of legal entry and permission to work in provisional status.

"Provisional status?" I asked. He told me a medical examination was required at my point of destination, following which I would be fully landed. With that the officer wished me luck, and disappeared. Given that most border immigration procedures lasted between 30 minutes and two hours, my 35 minutes was good.

The next morning I phoned TADP first thing. I called not only to express my thanks, but they needed input to be certain their information remained accurate and up to the minute. They also wanted to advise me of where to go for the medical exam. I thought any physician could do the tests, and indeed any doctor could, but they preferred their own people.

Located in a row of old, suburban town houses, coincidentally a half block from Tony and Judy's apartment, the free clinic looked like something out of Haight-Ashbury, with bells, pillows, beads, dyed spreads from India and the smell of sandalwood incense. The waiting room was probably once the front parlor of the old town house, the frost on the window dripping in the damp February air. The absence of three-piece suits evidenced that this was, after all, a free clinic. A girl in her early twenties, sitting in the corner, looked to have a drug problem; and one old man, I was sure, was homeless.

The tests were conducted by a surprisingly conventional-looking nurse, all in white, with the most important exam being the chest x-ray; tuberculosis was a big concern. To my dismay, the results of the exam would not be available for another two weeks, more time to worry.

Soon enough though, I was again sitting in the box-like waiting room. I did not wait long, because test results were all I was after and the nurse fit me in at the first opportunity.

In the doctor's office I found a long-haired man in his late thirties, wearing jeans, a farmer's shirt, and psychedelic suspenders. He was examining a little boy, apparently with swollen neck glands.

"You're here for test results, are you?" he said glancing over.

"Yes sir."

"Your name?"

"Simons."

While continuing to examine the little boy, he leaned over to a list on his desk.

"Donald Simons?"

"Yes," I answered, aware it was all down to this. Maybe the tests had revealed a problem I had not anticipated, a problem which would send me back to the States after all.

"Welcome to Canada," the doctor said with a broad smile.

I wondered how many of us he had said that to over the years. I thanked him, and quietly slipped out the door.

I assumed that doctor was Canadian, but later I learned he was also a landed immigrant from the United States. In private practice in Louisville, Kentucky for 14 years, he became disillusioned by the American culture, especially with middle-class housewives to whom he regularly prescribed headache pills and tranquilizers. Now he worked happily at the free clinic for a $100 a week.

Not long after receiving full immigration status, another letter came from my attorney. In it he described how he had spoken with at least eight other prominent lawyers about my case; all concurred that "reversible error" had been committed at my trial. A counselor for the Central Committee for Conscientious Objectors said, "I entirely agree. The handling of your case by the judge has been nothing short of appalling."

But to what end was this letter? Did he think I would come back, turn myself in and appeal? No. Nor did he ask me to in his letter, albeit it was a basis for returning if I wanted. Rather was it evidence that the loss of the trial was not his fault, in case I was thinking that. I was not. Actually, It seemed to me he was just as much a victim of the system as I was.

Having said that, I also now realized that from the standpoint of the cause of peace and justice, more was accomplished by our losing the case than by winning it. Had we won, the issue would have disappeared, whereas by losing, especially by being "railroaded" by the government, it continued in the minds and conversations of everyone touched by the case.

# CHAPTER NINE
## PUTTING IT BACK TOGETHER

Some exiles said Canada was like a prison, only with bigger walls. In time I might think so too, I supposed, after the initial shock of being there wore off. Meanwhile, that Canada was perceived by some as a prison meant attempting "furloughs," that is, sneaking back across the border from time to time. I could have tried it. When my father passed away I thought of going back for the funeral, but decided against it remembering his words to stay where I was. As it turned out, at the funeral my brother spotted a suspicious-looking car parked out front, two men studying all who came and went. This was how they got a lot of guys.

Periodically, an FBI agent would turn up at my mother's doorstep to verify my whereabouts, not that they would take her word alone. My mother described a typical encounter:

"Hello again, Mrs. Simons," the agent at the door would begin, after a couple days of surveillance to see if I might be back home. "I'm just doing another check," at which point he would show his identification to remind my mother who he was, though she knew very well who he was. It was always the same agent, and judging by her description of him, it was the man who arrested me.

"Come in," my mother would say, remembering the agent had to fill out some papers. Naturally, this whole process distressed and embarrassed her.

"This won't take long," the agent typically said as he sat on the edge of the sofa by the front window, my mother on the cushioned bench adjacent, the bench where I always used to sit when I was still living at home.

"Now then, Donald lives in Toronto, is that right?"

"Yes."

"That was Burnside Drive, wasn't it?"

"Yes."

"Can you give me the name of his current employer?" the agent would say looking up, "or is he still self-employed. House painting, wasn't it?"

"No. He has a new job. He's working for the Canadian Broadcasting Corporation."

"Really? How interesting. In what capacity?"

"He's a stagehand. He said he's just doing it temporarily, until he can get his career on track. He's got a Master's Degree you know."

"I know."

"I doubt there's much you don't know about him, sir."

"It's my job, Mrs. Simons. Too bad he got into all this trouble. He's a good clean-cut kid, from what I remember of him."

"He's a good boy."

The agent would then finish the form and say, "I won't take anymore of your time, Mrs. Simons. Sorry to have troubled you."

There was a time when Canada's renowned police agency, the Royal Canadian Mounted Police (RCMP), confirmed the whereabouts of U.S. draft law violators for the FBI. Tony was visited by a Mountie shortly after he took up residence in Toronto. Eventually, however, so many Americans were entering it became impossible to keep up. Nevertheless, throughout the late 60s and early 70s, the RCMP remained active in tracing American deserters.

One would think because of such things, there would be a special camaraderie among Americans in exile. In some cases it did exist, but to me, it seemed the exception. Most of us did not care to be reminded of our expatriate status; our goal, and the advice of TADP, was to start a new life, to disappear into Canadian society. Indeed, after the first few years, one was sufficiently Canadianized as to not think that much about the States. The psychological separation was apparent for me when I once visited Niagara Falls, Ontario and gazed across at the American flag on the opposite shore. I might just as well have been looking at an Australian flag, or Belgian; the same flag I used to pledge allegiance to now looked quite foreign. Despite the apparent lack of camaraderie, the fact remained that while individual circumstances for being there varied, we were united by the same experience; we were all Americans expatriated by the Vietnam War.

Psychological difficulties of one kind or another also seemed a common thread, and I had my share of suffering. For example, when I told my mother I was working as a CBC stagehand, and only temporarily until I could get my career on track, it was not the whole story. The truth was I had no career, cut off as I was after graduate school by my draft problems, and then the trial. In the process I lost all self-confidence, such that the further I got from the successes of my education, the more incapable I felt.

This was not to say I did not contribute to society, as during the year-and-a-half leading up to the trial and for my first few months in Canada, I did work; it was just that I was consistently underemployed. But the point was, I did not feel motivated beyond these things, so preoccupied and anxiety-plagued was I by my legal problems. Actually, I thought being in Canada would liberate me from my malaise, that with TADP's advice to "start life over," a new me would emerge and my confidence would return.

It proved quite the contrary; for subconsciously, at least, going to Canada represented yet another defeat in a series of defeats. Back in the States they were talking about "Post Traumatic Stress Disorder," among returning Vietnam veterans; I wondered if what I was feeling was akin. In short, I could not seem to "get my act together." Wearing an ever-present frown, I was not sleeping well, started drinking too much, and was frequently ill.

In fact, one night while drinking alone in my rented attic room I received a surprise phone call. One of the college professors who testified at my trial was in town with his teenage son and wanted to get together. Would I like to stop by the next night? Numbly, I said "Sure."

As it happened, I did not enjoy seeing him, his son, or their young Canadian friends, because they only reminded me of my troubles. Meanwhile, the professor explained how he would not let the draft get his son, and how he would move to Canada with the first threat. "That's nice," I said blankly, unfairly assuming he was patronizing me.

In an attempt to break free of my depression, I joined the Schooner Club of Toronto, whose meetings every Monday night at a downtown pub gave me a new circle of friends, the same way the Cafe had a few years earlier. As it happened, this connection resulted in three months of working on the club's new sixty-foot schooner in Nova Scotia, which several of us then sailed back to Toronto.

Determined to build on this fresh veneer of confidence, I decided to return to house painting for a few months, purely because I was good at it, something I needed to feel, and because I could be my own boss, also good for self-esteem. Even so, what I was going through at that time put a strain on my relationships with new Canadian friends. These people saw my run-in with the American draft and its consequences as my private business; when I talked about it, as I was inclined to do regularly in an attempt to purge myself of the poison, it was a case of telling them more than they cared to know.

"Really, old chap," interrupted the club president on one occasion, "you don't have to tell me all this."

"I'm sorry," I said, "I'll stop there. Except for one point. . . ." And with that I rambled on another 10 minutes.

"Trust me, old chap, I really prefer you wouldn't. . . ."

"But as if that was not bad enough . . . ," I continued. It was called embarrassing oneself.

Gradually, my mental health seemed to improve, as evidenced by a renewed interest in politics; I became particularly fascinated with the Canadian political and economic position on the Vietnam War.

The Canadian public opposed America's intervention in Southeast Asia. The Canadian government was not involved in the fighting, but continued arms shipments to the United States under a defense-sharing agreement. Not that America did not request greater Canadian involvement; indeed, other allies like Australia and New Zealand did send troops. Canadian Prime Minister Trudeau was reportedly opposed to sending troops due to his opposition to certain military methods used by America in Vietnam.

Nonetheless, he permitted the ongoing sale of military materiel. Under the Defense Production Sharing Agreement, Canada provided the United States $500 million worth of ammunition and military supplies for use in Vietnam, the profit from those sales contributing significantly to Canada's economy. It was clear, however, that the Prime Minister was walking a political tightrope. For example, at one point he confronted an appeal by 400 University of Toronto professors who wanted him to disassociate Canada from the war. Trudeau responded by saying: "For a broad range of reasons it is clear that an imposition of an embargo on the export of military equipment to the United States and concomitant termination of the Defense Production Sharing Agreements would have far reaching consequences that no Canadian government would contemplate with equanimity."[34]

Canada being in this position was a source of considerable frustration for many, especially younger Canadians, their perception of America's cultural and economic domination of Canada triggering a wave of increasingly strident Canadian nationalism. This growing spirit of nationalism was one of the first impressions I had on entering the country; I sensed I was welcome, yet not welcome. I was admired for my opposition to America's involvement in Vietnam, but was not totally accepted because I was an American.

The first place I noticed this reaction was at neighborhood grocery and variety stores. I frequented them enough for employees to know I was a new resident, and my age and accent were a tip-off. None of these people asked me directly whether I was in Canada because of the war, but their expressions and mannerisms, friendly but cool, communicated their feelings— I was just another part of the American invasion.

One man at the Schooner Club reminded me that there were Canadians who supported the involvement of the United States in Vietnam; I supposed he might have been a veteran of

34. Renee G. Kasinsky, *Refugees from Militarism: Draft-Age Americans In Canada* (New Brunswick, New Jersey: Transaction Publishers, 1976), p. 59.

the Canadian armed forces. Clearly, the impression he wanted me to have was that I was an inferior American, one who fled his country during wartime. But then, so that I did not think poorly of him for having that opinion, he would clasp me warmly on the back and tell a joke at the expense of Canadians.

For others, like my elderly landlady on Burnside Drive, I was simply a curiosity. She had seen reports on television about American "draft-dodgers" and deserters taking refuge in Canada. When I went to see the room for rent, one of the first things she asked was, "Are you a dodger?" Not wanting to explain it all to her, I simply said, "Yes." Her eyes grew wide as she smiled.

On the other hand, some Canadians were just plain defensive. One said, "We have history and politics here too, you know." This seemed less to do with anything I said about the United States, than a reaction to my not asking more about Canada's heritage and traditions.

Nevertheless, I sometimes detected a sort of inferiority complex among Canadians vis-a-vis the United States. This amazed me, because I found Canada superior to America in many ways. Canada had a low crime rate, nonmilitaristic attitudes, a clean environment, a diversity of ethnic groups encouraged to maintain their identities, socialized medicine, and an innovativeness and progressiveness like nothing I had seen before. When one man told me flat out, "Canada is superior to the United States," I did not disagree.

Some Canadians did take issue with American draft law violators not only being permitted safe refuge in Canada, but being granted landed-immigrant status as well. However, the precedence for this, as many of them knew, was apparent in their history books.

French-Canadians, for instance, always had an aversion to conscription; the idea of fighting Britain's imperial wars never appealed to them. Indeed, during World War I and World War II, tens of thousands of French-Canadians refused to register for the Canadian draft and rioted in the streets. The mayor of Montreal was jailed from 1940 to 1944 for openly encouraging draft resistance. A popular figure, he was reelected from jail. After World War II, with the support of labor and other groups, the French-Canadian resistance led to the end of conscription in all of Canada.

In addition, the admission of immigrants who had refused military service in their native countries was one of Canada's oldest traditions. Ironically, it was also a tradition in the United States, where many European draft resisters and deserters found refuge on American shores. Canada, like the United States, also had a custom of welcoming political refugees from other countries, although Canada was quick to point out that it did not consider American draft law violators in that category.

Draft resisting Americans were also taken in simply because of Canada's open immigration policy. Canada was a very large country with proportionately few inhabitants; it could always use manpower, especially young Americans who were typically well-educated and skilled. Indeed, during the Vietnam War, many were very well-educated, and highly skilled.

Nevertheless, some members of the Canadian Parliament were not too happy with this arrangement, especially regarding the entry of American military deserters. Note this exchange:

Member of Parliament: In reference to deserters from the United States I asked the Minister of Manpower and Immigration whether he was aware of the fact that deserters from the United States army are more or less criminals. I now direct my question to the Prime Minister.

Prime Minister: I think the honorable member had better put the "more or less" back in there—perhaps more of the "less" than of the "more."[35]

The Canadian attitude toward American draft resisters and deserters also took into consideration how we existed as a community and in the society in general. For example, while my assimilation into Canadian culture was largely personal and private, there was more kinship for many others. In Toronto, for instance, there was a collection of American com-

35. Kasinsky, p. 65.

munes which were havens for American draft violators and deserters. Several were located in what was known as the "lower village" in the area of Spadina and University Avenues, and College and Huron Streets. The University of Toronto campus and Rochdale College were also in this vicinity. Rochdale College was basically a residence for the University of Toronto, but in the spirit of the 60s, it became a "do your own thing" college. It did not grant degrees; yet it was recognized as an educational institution by the Province of Ontario.

One of the Canadians who was closely associated with Rochdale College was editor of the aforementioned *Manual for Draft-Age Immigrants to Canada*. He told me its first edition was published in January 1968 and sold 5,000 copies. The second printing, published two months later sold 20,000 copies, with 65,000 sold by 1970.

The manual's information was invaluable to those of us in need, especially since it included a list of Canadian support groups like TADP. Toronto had seven others, some of which were specialized like the Black Refugee Committee, and the Jewish Immigrant Aid Service. Vancouver had two, the Committee to Aid American War Objectors, and the American Deserters Committee; Regina, Saskatchewan also had two, similarly defined. Halifax, Saint John, Quebec City, Guelph, Kitchener, London, Thunder Bay, Welland, Windsor, Winona, Winnipeg, Saskatoon, Calgary, and Victoria, also had assistance groups.

Various underground publications such as *Harbinger, Guerrilla,* and *The American Expatriate in Canada* were also found in Toronto's lower village. Newspapers of the left, they contained political commentary, uncensored information about the war and news of the continuing antiwar movement in the United States and abroad. They also provided assistance to Americans including details about Canadian life, places to stay, temporary jobs, and counseling services.

Natural food stores and "head shops" that featured countercultural clothes and supplies could also be found there, and many of these shops were owned by local communal families. It was rumored that on some blocks, apartments and basements were occupied only by Americans.

By contrast, the circle I traveled in can be exemplified by a social occasion in the old residential area of Rosedale. Present were four couples and myself, ranging in age from early 20s to early 30s. Three of the men were American exiles, the other two, sympathetic young members of the Canadian intelligentsia. Except for my Toronto contact Tony, who had longish hair, we looked like junior executives.

In this regard it was disappointing to me that anytime the television media, especially the American networks, wanted to do a story on the exiles in Canada, they always wound up with the same four or five members of the resident counterculture, as though they had been elected spokesmen. When I entered the country it was estimated that there were thousands of us, exact figures being impossible to determine; but these same guys always seemed to be interviewed. It gave the impression to Americans and Canadians alike that we were predominantly a radical fringe, when in truth we were a cross section of young Americans.

One reason the same few always appeared was that the majority did not care to be interviewed, or so I surmised. People had various reasons for keeping to themselves. For example, some did not want to risk jeopardizing landed status; for others, leaving the States was traumatic enough, they did not want to rehash it; and probably for most, the goal was to disappear into Canadian society and to start life over. America was past history.

I bided my time being a painter for the final months of my first year in Canada. Being in the Schooner Club was good for me, but I needed to find work to match. Forcing the issue was that the dead of winter had me all but unemployed. Finally, an acquaintance at the club led me to the job at the Canadian Broadcast Corporation. As mentioned, I was a stagehand, a job for which I was amply qualified due to my experience in technical theater in college. However, it was still underemployment, so I considered it only "temporary."

Naturally, I was jubilant over the signing of the Vietnam peace treaty on January 27, 1973, but there was one thing that bothered me. Was it only a coincidence that the war was winding down just at the close of President Nixon's first term in office, Secretary of State Henry Kissinger declaring "Peace is at hand," just before the November elections? Did not that, coupled with the promise of the end of draft calls as of December 1972, all but guarantee Nixon's reelection? As it happened, he won by a landslide.

In 1973 my brother moved to Toronto, something I did not understand and he did not explain. I wanted to think he did this to show solidarity with me, although I suspected it had equally to do with his own contracting business not going well, and the passing the year before of our father; perhaps he felt isolated.

Then again he was impressed by Toronto when he and my mother paid a visit the previous year, even though the most memorable event during that trip was the three of us riding back south, with me having to get out at the border. The sadness and frustration surrounding that incident might also have contributed to my brother's northward move.

The issue of amnesty arose from time to time, but having erected a psychological wall, I chose to not give it much thought; why put hope into something that unlikely? In fact, the issue did surface soon after my arrival in Canada. From my journal:

> January 17, 1972: Today I purchased the latest issue of *Newsweek* magazine, which was featuring a special article on the amnesty question. With the reading of this, I am convinced unconditional amnesty will never be granted; the article said there are some 75,000 of us here now, the greater percentage of whom would not accept a conditional amnesty, I am sure. I am among them. A conditional amnesty would mean our admitting our guilt in refusing to support an illegal and immoral war. The fact is, we are not guilty. We are right. But the U.S. government will never admit that.

Still the article contained interesting information: Senator Robert Taft, an Ohio Republican not renowned for liberal causes, had recently proposed a bill that would clear draft law violators of any offense, provided they were willing to perform three years of alternative public service; Manhattan Representative Edward Koch was also pursuing the issue. A growing variety of organizations including the National Council of Churches, the American Civil Liberties Union, and the War Resisters League, were pressing the same cause.

Moreover, there was talk that amnesty might become a significant campaign issue in 1972, George McGovern having spoken up for unconditional amnesty and John Lindsay endorsing a conditional version. President Nixon, who had earlier dismissed the notion with a curt "No," was now taking a more magnanimous position. In a national television interview with CBS correspondent Dan Rather, he said, "We always, under our system, provide amnesty . . . I for one would be very liberal with regard to amnesty, but not while there are Americans in Vietnam fighting to serve their country . . . and not while POWs are held by the enemy. After that, we would consider it . . ."

The article went on to explain how the public at large was by no means as hostile to amnesty as might have been supposed at that stage of the war. A special nationwide poll conducted for *Newsweek* by the Gallup Organization found that when the question was posed in general terms—whether or not to grant amnesty to young men who had left the country to avoid the draft—only 28 percent were in favor while 58 percent stood opposed. But when the issue was refined to include the possibility of amnesty on condition of some period of public service, only 22 percent remained in opposition. An overwhelming 63 percent favored conditional amnesty, and an additional 7 percent believed there should be no service requirement; 1 percent were not sure whether conditions should be attached. Therefore, a total of 71 percent favored amnesty in some form. Among that group, 37 percent favored immediate amnesty.

The survey found women somewhat more inclined to favor amnesty than men; the same was true of people under 40 as compared to their elders. Veterans, and those whose families included a veteran, tended to be more opposed to the idea.

The *Newsweek* poll also found that support for First Lieutenant William Calley remained strong. When asked whether amnesty should be granted to Calley and other Americans convicted of war crimes in Vietnam, a strong plurality of 49 percent was in favor; only 24 percent opposed.

Even though President Nixon expressed a willingness to consider amnesty, he did not get a chance to follow through. Accused of covering up impropriety during the 1972 campaign, he was forced to resign over the Watergate scandal; Vice President Gerald Ford succeeded him.

In 1974, President Ford presented his limited clemency plan for draft law violators and deserters; a close look revealed how unacceptable it was, some called it insulting. Ford proposed a program that called for exiles to turn themselves in and serve "alternative service" as a means of "earned reentry" into American society, as though we were guilty of wrongdoing and clambering at the border, desperate to return.

Still, some took advantage of the program. To them it was a question of priorities, and being back in the States came first. For most of us though, it was a matter of principle, some even called for a full apology from the American government. Meanwhile, I suspected there would not be any real solution until it was politically advantageous to an American President.

There was another reason the Ford program had a bad taste to it. On August 8, 1974 President Ford granted an unconditional pardon to Richard Nixon for "any federal crimes he committed or may have committed while in office," an action that prompted a great deal of criticism from liberals and conservatives alike. Perhaps as an attempt to quiet the liberals, Ford introduced his clemency plan just eight days later.

Apparently, Ford did not see how offensive this was. He had given a full pardon to a man many were calling a "crook," while offering only a conditional amnesty, with penalties, to those acting on moral grounds against a war now generally conceded as a legal and ethical disaster. No wonder the offer was all but ignored.

Meanwhile, the final chapter to America's misadventure in Vietnam came in 1975. It was marked by the collapse of the Saigon government and the subsequent airlift of all remaining Americans and many South Vietnamese supporters. Draft registration also ended in 1975.

Another year and a half would pass before the matter of the exiles resurfaced, this time in the form of a campaign promise by Presidential candidate Jimmy Carter. His proposed pardon was something of a puzzle. On television I watched Carter discuss the pardon at a veteran's convention. The response was so overwhelmingly negative I wondered why, if he wanted to be elected, he even mentioned it at all.

This may have been the reason the amnesty issue was only briefly discussed in the Ford-Carter presidential debates. During the first debate Ford stated:

> I am against an across-the-board pardon of draft evaders or military deserters . . . I gave in September of 1974 an opportunity for all draft evaders, all deserters to come in voluntarily—clear their records by earning an opportunity to restore their good citizenship . . . I don't think we should go any further.

Carter's position was:

> I think it's very difficult for President Ford to explain the difference between the pardon of President Nixon and his attitude toward those who violated the draft laws . . . I don't advocate amnesty; I advocate pardon. There's a difference . . . amnesty means that what you did was right. Pardon means that what you did, whether it's right or wrong, you're forgiven for it . . . I think that now is the time to heal our country after the Vietnam War.[36]

Notably, Carter's proposed pardon applied only to draft law violators, not to deserters who were by far the larger group; Ford's program, on the other hand, also included deserters.

There was no telling what would have happened to us had Ford lost the 1976 Republican nomination to challenger Ronald Reagan; Mr. Reagan had come down hard on Carter's promised pardon. As it was, Carter just narrowly defeated Ford.

Because the amnesty issue was kept in the background toward the end of the campaign, and even after the elections, I doubted whether President-elect Carter would actually do anything. But he signed the pardon into law the day after his

36. *U.S. News and World Report*, October 4, 1976, pp. 14–15.

inauguration. I had the sense that he had to do this quickly; I got the impression that if he did not do it right away, during the "honeymoon" of his Presidency, he would never have gotten away with it.

Ironically, the precedent of Ford's full pardon of Nixon might have made the exile pill easier for the American public to swallow. It was not an easy pill for exiles to swallow however, especially for those of us who thought what we had done was morally correct. From my journal:

January 21, 1977. At this moment, I am watching a news program which has announced that President Carter, inaugurated only yesterday, has granted a pardon to all draft law violators. I have mixed emotions, my immediate response being regret. For months to come now, this decision will bring much bitter reaction in the U.S.; note Senator Barry Goldwater, who has called the pardon a "disgrace." "Regrettable," is the response from the VFW and American Legion. The governor of New Hampshire was so disgusted he ordered state flags flown at half-staff. What am I to feel?

Meanwhile, *The American Exile in Canada* has published their opinion that the pardon does not go far enough, that it should include military deserters. I agree. But my agreement is from the standpoint that the Vietnam War and everything connected with it was ugly and sad, and as such, the slate should be cleared once and for all.

Beyond this, I think it is generally the case for those of us who have been in Canada a number of years now, to be distrustful of the pardon. So firm is the mental block regarding crossing the border, the impulse is to resist the idea. I am wary of some legal land mine. I am suspicious of some "small print" which would send me back to trial and ultimately to prison. I think it is an apprehension all of us here feel.

But then my strongest emotional reaction regards the U.S. families who lost their sons in Vietnam. A part of me wants to feel guilty for still being alive. The draft board tried to make me feel guilty by telling me that each time I refused induction, some other guy went in my place.

But why should I feel guilty for what was right? Vietnam was an illegal and immoral war. Am I to be blamed for knowing the truth? Still I cannot deny my strong feelings for the families who lost their sons, many of them my friends. To them I say I'm sorry. But I will not apologize for being right.

I expressed these feelings to a co-worker, a stagehand fresh from Texas. On learning I was an exile, he asked if I was going back.

"No, I don't think so," I said. "Why would I put myself through all that? Too many people back there think we're the scum of the earth. I don't need that."

He looked over. "I think you'd find a lot of attitudes have changed."

Shortly after Carter's announcement I received three letters. One was from my West Virginia attorney, the second from my draft counselor in Pittsburgh, and a third from the federal court. The latter read:

On December 13 and 14, 1971, the defendant, DONALD LAIRD SIMONS, was tried and found guilty by a jury for failing and refusing to submit to induction in the Armed Forces of the United States, in violation of Title 50 App., Section 462(A), United States Code. On January 28, 1972, the defendant failed to appear for subsequent post-trial proceedings and a bench warrant was issued for the defendant on February 10, 1972.

Pursuant to the Presidential Pardon issued on January 21, 1977 by President Jimmy Carter, the United States hereby moves the Court for an Order setting aside the defendant's conviction and dismissing the Indictment with prejudice [meaning I could not be indicted again for the same charges] and withdrawing the outstanding bench warrant. It is therefore ORDERED that the defendant's conviction in this case be set aside, that the Indictment be dismissed with prejudice, and the bench warrant issued on February 10, 1972 be withdrawn.

This was signed by the judge, and endorsed by the district attorney.

On reading these words, I had a different sense of it all. Put simply, I felt relieved. I avoided the temptation to somehow feel victorious, or otherwise vindicated. I simply felt relieved. Unexpectedly, these words also made the idea of going back look different. But why should I go back? After all, I had been successful in creating a new Donald Simons, a Canadian Donald Simons, who now felt secure and was at peace. Living modestly in a pleasant high-rise apartment building in cosmopolitan downtown Toronto, I could even walk to my job in 15 minutes. As for CBC television, I had gone from stagehand to apprentice rigger, and were I to stay I could move into management. Not a bad situation.

The problem with all this was revealed to me one day as I drove along frozen Lakeshore Boulevard. For perspective I pulled into the parking lot of the little motel where I stayed that first night in Canada five years earlier. As I gazed out at the bare trees and frozen shoreline, lean sea gulls strutting about bravely in the icy wind, suddenly I saw what my life had been from my first day in Canada to that very moment—I had been incarcerated. Canada had been a prison, only with bigger walls, like some had said. I had not chosen to be there of my own free will; I was forced there. No matter that I had a Canadian flag decal in my car window in place of the American one, the fact remained I was still an American in exile.

I glanced down at the court order in my lap, again reading how the charges against me had been dropped. What timing, I thought. It was five years to the month since I had entered Canada, meaning I was now eligible for Canadian citizenship.

I sighed and looked out again to the lake, a scene I had come to know like the back of my hand. Indeed, there was much I knew about Canada and had come to love over those five years. I had a lot of friends there now, more friends than I had at any other time in my life. In many ways I had blossomed in Canada, had "come of age" there; it was a far richer life than I could ever have known in Morgantown, West Virginia.

## PUTTING IT BACK TOGETHER

I decided to go back to Morgantown for a visit and did so two months later. I took an airplane rather than my car because of the mental block I had about crossing the border; I did not want to get down there and panic. Taking the plane worked fine until the first stop, Cleveland, where I looked out the window only to see rows of military planes. "How fitting," I said out loud, the person in the next seat glancing over at me. But it did not end there. When I got to Pittsburgh, where I was to transfer to a commuter plane for the final 60 miles down to Morgantown, there were even more military planes, their drab green, brown, and gray camouflage etched menacingly along the airport perimeter. During the entire time I was in Canada, I did not see one militaristic scene; now suddenly I was reminded where I was again. Once more I felt the anger rise in me, all the old antiwar feelings flooding back; it was all I could do to keep from grabbing the next plane back to Toronto. But I made it that far, and I knew how important it was to go through this. As it turned out, I was practically the only one on the Morgantown plane and happily, the only one in the cab as it pulled up in front of the family homestead.

Peering out, my eyes misted as I looked on the house I thought I would never see again; I flashed back to the last view of it I had five years prior when I looked through the icy window of my brother's truck. Entering the house I received the welcome home of my mother, the only one there, a welcome home born more of relief than of pride. But there was plenty of joy for me, as to my surprise I was suddenly up and down the stairs and out around the yard like a puppy in a new home. Then upstairs in my old room, I gazed from a sunny front window which had known me all my life.

Yet despite this coming full circle, I returned to Canada where I lived happily for another year and a half. Then, in July 1978 I did return to the American West Coast, there to resume graduate studies, this time without the war and without the draft.

# AFTERWORD

This record would not be complete without a word about adjustment problems I experienced as a returning exile. The greatest source of suffering was the return of paranoia, especially during visits to my hometown; it got so bad that I dreaded leaving the house. I remained convinced that it was right to refuse induction and go into exile, but I was sure many in town felt the opposite; so I envisioned potentially ugly scenes at every encounter.

Certain family members and friends remained cool towards me which, of course, was distressing; they still thought I had done something wrong. For instance, my relatives on the West Coast did not communicate with me for six years; they did not wish me luck with my trial and did not have so much as a syllable for me until after the Carter pardon.

I also became very distrustful of government authority and bureaucrats, so that the simple act of validating my American driver's license had me reading the fine print four or five times. But it ran deeper than that and included a distrust of emotions surrounding love of country, and feelings of patriotism. Where I once was misty-eyed at the playing of the *Star Spangled Banner*, I now felt only anger. I knew full well the power government symbols had over people and what they could lead to; this awareness and the bitterness that accompanied it continued for years.

Finally, I was depressed by the realization that nothing really had changed in America, nothing had been learned. Three years after granting pardons to draft law violators, President Carter reinstated the draft. Once again, all 18-year-old males were required by law to register for the draft or face five years in prison and a $10,000 fine. The reinstatement of the draft was most discouraging for me because it was a signal to the world that the United States was "reloading," and that the people of the world, especially young people in our country had better watch out.

More recently, the so-called victory of American and Allied forces in the Persian Gulf War resulted in a celebration of militarism not seen since World War II. If history is any measure, this celebration of militarism surely will lead to another war.

My advice to young people facing induction is to simply follow your heart. You can refuse. If your heart tells you that it is wrong to kill, then refuse to do it. If you do not listen to the wisdom of your heart, you may suffer for the rest of your days. However, if you are true to yourself and reject the weapons thrust into your hands, you may suffer in the short run, but you will forever be at peace.

# APPENDIX
## THE VIETNAM WAR: AN OVERVIEW

At the end of World War II, Vietnamese nationalist and Communist groups sought to achieve independence despite France's efforts to reestablish colonial rule over Cambodia, Laos, and Vietnam. The strongest of the Vietnamese nationalist groups was Ho Chi Minh's Communist-led "Vietminh," the abbreviated name for the League for the Independence of Vietnam.

On September 2, 1945 Ho declared Vietnam independent and announced the creation of the Democratic Republic of Vietnam (DRVN). The French recognized the DRVN on March 6, 1946 "as a free state within the French union." However, a series of blunders and misunderstandings by both sides led to armed conflict and the beginning of the French-Vietminh war on December 19, 1946.

As the war continued, the French sought non-Communist support by turning to the former Emperor of Vietnam, Bao Dai, in hopes of rallying the Vietnamese populace. With French approval, on July 1, 1949 Bao formed the "State of Vietnam" with its capital in Saigon.

The United States recognized the new state on February 7, 1950; to assist it, President Truman announced on June 27th that America was sending a 35-man Military Assistance Advisory Group to instruct troops in the use of American weapons. Other assistance soon followed; on December 23, 1950 a Mutual Defense Assistance Agreement was signed and on

September 7, 1951 direct economic assistance to the Saigon government began.

On May 8, 1954 the French stronghold of Dien Bien Phu in Northern Vietnam fell to Communist forces; on the same date a Geneva Conference on Indochina commenced attended by France, Britain, Russia, the United States, the Democratic Republic of Vietnam, the State of Vietnam, Laos, Cambodia and Communist China. At that conference, France and the DRVN agreed to a partition of Vietnam along the 17th parallel, a ban on new troops or bases and the scheduling of reunification elections in July 1956. The parties also agreed to the creation of an International Control Commission comprised of India, Canada, and Poland to supervise the implementation of the agreement. The United States and the State of Vietnam did not sign.

On October 24, 1954 President Eisenhower offered the Saigon government economic aid, agreeing four months later to train the South Vietnamese Army. On October 23, 1955 a South Vietnamese national referendum deposed Bao Dai and created a republic with Ngo Dinh Diem as its first president. Diem then announced that unification elections as specified by the Geneva Conference were impossible due to intimidation by North Vietnam.

Two years later, on October 22, 1957 the first injuries among American military advisors were reported; the first American casualties in a combat situation reportedly occurred on July 8, 1959. Upon South Vietnam's request, the United States increased the number of military advisers from 327 to 685 in May, 1960. In October of the same year, President Eisenhower announced continued assistance to South Vietnam; two months later North Vietnam announced the formation of the National Liberation Front, whereupon guerrilla warfare increased in the South.

On April 3, 1961 the Kennedy Administration signed the Treaty of Amity and Economic Relations with South Vietnam. That year Kennedy declared the United States was prepared to help the Republic "preserve its independence." A June 2, 1962 report from the International Control Commission provided evidence that North Vietnam was supporting, organizing, and carrying out hostile acts in the South; by the end of the year American forces increased to 4,000. The assassination of President Diem in 1963 resulted in a series of coups as American troop strength grew to 15,000.

In August 1964, the United States' destroyers *Maddox* and *C. Turner Joy* were reportedly attacked by North Vietnamese torpedo boats in the Gulf of Tonkin; President Johnson immediately ordered retaliatory attacks. Within days, the United States Congress approved the Gulf of Tonkin Resolution giving the president the power to "take all necessary measures to repel any armed attack against the forces of the United States and to prevent further aggression." American forces were increased to 23,000.

In February 1965, the United States began bombing raids over North Vietnam and on June 8th, the President authorized American commanders to send ground forces into combat. Soon after, President Johnson increased troop strength to 125,000; the increases would continue until April 1969 when they reached a high of 543,400.

Several other nations also sent troops to support South Vietnam. South Korea became involved due to their close association with the United States since the Korean War; Thailand sent troops because of their distrust of Communist intentions in the region; Australia and New Zealand committed forces as a result of their charter membership in the Southeast Asia Treaty Organization and their interest in the security of the region.

President Nixon began withdrawing American troops in 1969 as part of the so-called "Vietnamization" program, returning the burden of the fighting to the South Vietnamese Army. When a peace treaty was finally signed on January 27, 1973 only 23,000 American troops remained.

Still, the original war between South Vietnam's government, the Vietcong and the North Vietnamese continued until 1975, when South Vietnam fell and the country was unified.[37]

During the main period of hostilities (August 1964-January 1973), some 8,744,000 Americans served in the military, making the Vietnam War second only to World War II in the

37. *New York Times*, May 1, 1975, pp. 17–20; May 17, 1975, p. 27; Stanley Karnow, *Vietnam: A History* (New York: Viking, 1983), pp. 670–686.

number of personnel involved. However, because of the constant rotation of servicemen, generally a one year tour of duty, a greater percentage of Vietnam-era servicemen spent time in Vietnam.

African-Americans comprised about 13 percent of the total troop force in Vietnam, approximately the proportion of blacks in the United States at the time; however, 28 percent had combat assignments, yet only 2 percent of the officers were black.[38]

The American military lost over 47,000 men in combat, more than 10,000 others died from aircraft accidents and various other causes; there were 313,616 wounded, of which 153,300 were classified as seriously wounded. Of the seriously wounded, 82 percent were saved (compared to 71 percent in World War II, and 74 percent in Korea); the higher percentage was attributed to the extensive use of helicopters for evacuation and the advanced medical facilities available. While only 2.6 percent of those who reached hospitals died, some 10,000 servicemen lost at least one limb (more than all those in World War II and Korea combined), the result of the use of booby traps, mines, ambushes, and other guerilla tactics. Only a small percentage of servicemen actually fought against large Vietcong or North Vietnamese units, but many had direct exposure to the war's deadly effects; approximately 75 percent were targets of mortars or rockets, and 56 percent witnessed a comrade being killed or wounded.

South Vietnam reported 185,528 killed and 499,026 wounded; North Vietnam and the Vietcong were said to have lost 924,048 in combat. An estimated 415,000 Vietnamese civilians were killed in the war, with over 935,000 wounded. Other casualties included, 4,407 troops from South Korea, and 350 Thais; Australia and New Zealand lost 475, with 2,348 wounded.

There were 8 million tons of bombs dropped over North Vietnam, South Vietnam, Laos, and Cambodia, or four times the tonnage for all of World War II; in Laos alone between 1965 and 1971, 2,236,000 tons of bombs were dropped on infil-

38. John S. Bowman, ed., *The Vietnam War: An Almanac* (New York: World Almanac Publications, 1985), p. 358.

tration routes, such as the Ho Chi Minh Trail, which fed troops and supplies to the war in the South.

It was roughly, but reasonably estimated that the war cost the United States $150 billion dollars in direct expenses; other costs, such as payments to veterans and interest on debts incurred, are all but unending.

On another front, the war produced massive disaffection in the military and civilian sectors as evidenced, in part, by desertion incidents and prosecution for draft resistance. The total number of desertions exceeded 550,000; over 100,000 men were discharged for absence without leave and desertion. Of those, 5,000 were "in country" desertions; 32,000 involved failure to report for duty in Vietnam, refusal to return from rest and relaxation breaks, and unauthorized absences after completing a tour of duty in Vietnam.[39]

The number of draft offenders was estimated at over 570,000; this includes 250,000 men who never registered for the draft, 110,000 others who violated Selective Service law in some fashion, but were never charged with a crime, and 210,000 men formally accused as draft offenders. Most in the latter group were not prosecuted; ultimately, only 25,000 men were indicted for draft law violations; 8,750 were convicted, and 4,000 imprisoned.[40]

The exact number of deserters and draft resisters who fled the country is unknown. Inexact estimates, based on extrapolations from Canadian immigration data, suggest that over 40,000 draft resisters and deserters fled the country during the Vietnam era. Most went to Canada, but some 10,000 fled to other countries, especially Sweden and Mexico.[41]

During the war, due process rights for draft registrants were expanded in accordance with decisions reached by the Supreme Court. By 1972, twelve significant changes in the administration of the draft law appeared. Major ones included

39. James S. Olson, ed., *Dictionary of the Vietnam War* (New York: Greenwood Press, 1988). p. 115.
40. Lawrence Baskir and William Strauss, *Chance and Circumstance: The Draft, the War, and the Vietnam Generation* (New York: Alfred A. Knopf, 1978), pp. 5, 69.
41. Kohn, p. 92; *U.S. News and World Report*, January 31, 1977, p. 22; Baskir and Strauss, pp. 115, 169.

the right to bring witnesses to a personal appearance before the board and the right to a personal appearance as part of an appeal. Local boards and appeal boards were also required to give registrants the reasons why a request for a classification was denied.[42]

Some of the most important changes involved conscientious objector classifications. When the Vietnam War began, only those opposed to all wars on the basis of "religious training and belief" could obtain CO status. However, in two important Supreme Court cases, the right to objector status was enlarged to include atheists and agnostics, despite the statute's "religious" specification.

In the first case, *U.S. v. Seeger* (1965),[43] the high court held that a registrant was no longer required to base his claim on a belief in a God or a "Supreme Being"; it was sufficient to have a "sincere or meaningful belief" which occupied a place "parallel to that filled by God." In the second case, *Welsh v. U.S.* (1970),[44] the court reaffirmed the Seeger decision and explicitly included strongly held "moral" or "ethical" beliefs as adequate in meeting the test for CO status.

During the Vietnam era, a total of 172,000 men received I-O conscientious objector status from the Selective Service.[45] Since classification I-A and I-A-O were combined to reflect those available for induction, no statistics were published on the number of men who entered the military as I-A-O conscientious objectors.

Three other court rulings were central during the period; these pertained to "selective prosecution" of draft opponents who found themselves subject to extralegal government surveillance and prosecution.

In *Oestereich v. Selective Service* (1968),[46] the court held that the Selective Service could not reclassify an otherwise exempt person in retaliation for participation in antiwar protests. The Supreme Court voided the reclassification of a divinity stu-

42. Kohn, p. 113.
43. *U.S. v. Seeger*, 380 U.S. 163 (1965).
44. *Welch v. U.S.*, 389 U.S. 333 (1970).
45. Baskir and Strauss, p. 30.
46. *Ostereich v. Selective Service*, 393 U.S. 233 (1968).

dent who mailed in his draft registration card as a protest against the Vietnam War.

In *Gutknecht v. U.S.* (1970),[47] the court ruled against the Selective Service in a case of accelerated induction. To protest the war, David Earl Gutknecht returned his registration certificate only to have his local board accelerate his induction date, assigning him "first priority in the order of induction," and placing his name ahead of many other nonprotesting potential inductees. The court struck down this practice stating that illegal protest activity was to be addressed by criminal procedures and not by internal Selective Service means. In the ruling the court stated that the Selective Service System was not a "freewheeling agency meting out their own brand of justice in a vindictive manner."

Finally, in *U.S. v. Falk* (1975),[48] an active member of a draft resistance organization was indicted and convicted in a federal court for nonpossession of a draft card, an offense that was rarely prosecuted. Jeffrey Falk appealed his conviction on the grounds of illegal selective prosecution, convinced that the real reason he was arrested was his draft counseling activity. The Court of Appeals agreed and his conviction was overturned; they found there was substantial evidence that he was selected for prosecution in violation of his constitutionally protected right to free speech.

47. *Gutknecht v. U.S.*, 396 U.S. 296 (1970).
48. *U.S v. Falk*, 479 F.2d 616 (1973).

# SELECTED BIBLIOGRAPHY

Anderson, Martin, ed. *Conscription: A Select and Annotated Bibliography.* Stanford, California: Hoover Institution Press, 1976.
_____. *Registration and the Draft.* Stanford, California: Hoover Institution Press, 1982.
Baskir, Lawrence, and Strauss, William. *Chance and Circumstance: The Draft, the War, and the Vietnam Generation.* New York: Knopf, 1978.
Berrigan, Daniel. *No Bars to Manhood.* Garden City, New Jersey: Doubleday, 1970.
_____. *The Trial of the Cantonsville Nine.* Boston: Beacon Press, 1970.
Bowman, John S., ed. *The Vietnam War: An Almanac.* New York: World Almanac Publications, 1985.
Burtchaell, James T., ed. *A Just War No Longer Exists: The Teaching and Trial of Don Lorenzo Milani.* Notre Dame, Indiana: University of Notre Dame Press, 1988.
Chambers, John W., II. *To Raise an Army: The Draft Comes to Modern America.* New York: Free Press, 1987.
Chan, Wing-tsit. *The Way of Lao Tzu.* New York: Bobbs-Merrill 1963.
Childress, James F. *Moral Responsibility in Conflicts: Essays on Nonviolence, War, and Conscience.* Baton Rouge, Louisiana: Louisiana State University Press, 1982.
Clifford, J. Garry, and Spencer, Samuel R., Jr. *The First Peacetime Draft.* Lawrence, Kansas: University of Kansas Press, 1986.
Coffin, William S., Jr., and Leibman, Morris I. *Civil Disobedience: Aid or Hindrance to Justice.* Washington, D.C.: American Enterprise Institute for Public Policy Research, 1972.

Cohen, Eliot A. *Citizens and Soldiers: The Dilemmas of Military Service.* Ithaca, New York: Cornell University Press, 1985.

Committee for Economic Development. *Military Manpower and National Security.* New York: Committee for Economic Development, 1972.

*Conscientious Objection to Military Service.* New York: United Nations, 1985.

Cooney, Robert, and Michalowski, Helen. eds. *The Power of the People: Active Nonviolence in the United States.* Philadelphia: New Society Publishers, 1987.

Curry, G. David. *Sunshine Patriots: Punishment and the Vietnam Offender.* Notre Dame, Indiana: University of Notre Dame Press, 1985.

DeBenedetti, Charles and Chatfield, Charles. *An American Ordeal: The Antiwar Movement of the Vietnam Era.* Syracuse, New York: Syracuse University Press.

Dellinger, David. *Revolutionary Nonviolence: Essays.* Indianapolis, Indiana: Bobbs-Merrill, 1970.

Doherty, William T., and Summers, Festus P. *West Virginia University: Symbol of Unity in a Sectionalized State.* Morgantown, West Virginia: West Virginia University Press, 1982.

Drescher, John M. *Why I am a Conscientious Objector.* Scottdale, Pennsylvania: Herald Press, 1982.

*Fighting Back: Lesbian and Gay Draft, Military and Veterans Issues.* New York: National Lawyers Guild, 1984.

Finney, Torin R. *Unsung Hero of the Great War: The Life and Witness of Ben Salmon.* Mahwah, New Jersey: Paulist Press, 1989.

Flynn, George Q. *Lewis B. Hershey, Mr. Selective Service.* Chapel Hill, North Carolina: University of North Carolina Press, 1985.

French, Paul C. *We Won't Murder: Being the Story of Men Who Followed Their Conscientious Scruples and Helped Give Life to Democracy.* Englewood, New Jersey: Ozer Press, 1972.

Fullinwider, Robert K., ed. *Conscripts and Volunteers: Military Requirements, Social Justice and the All-Volunteer Force.* Lanham, Maryland: Rowman, 1983.

Gandhi, Mohandas K. *Autobiography: The Story of My Experiments With Truth.* New York: Dover Publications, 1983.

Gaylin, Willard. *In Service of Their Country: War Resisters in Prison.* New York: Viking Press, 1970.

Gioglio, Gerald R. *Days of Decision: An Oral History of Conscientious Objectors in the Military During the Vietnam War.* Trenton, New Jersey: Broken Rifle Press, 1989.

# SELECTED BIBLIOGRAPHY

Gitlin, Todd. *The Sixties: Years of Hope, Days of Rage.* New York: Bantam, 1987.

Goodpoaster, Andrew J., and Elliott, Lloyd H. *Toward a Consensus on Military Service.* New Brunswick, New Jersey: Transaction Books, 1983.

Graham, John R. *Constitutional History of the Military Draft.* Minneapolis, Minnesota: Ross and Haines, 1971.

Graham, John W. *Conscription and Conscience: A History 1916–1919.* New York: Kelley Publishers, 1969.

Granatstein, J. L. *Broken Promises: A History of Conscription in Canada.* New York: Oxford University Press, 1977.

Halstead, Fred. *Out Now! A Participant's Account of the American Movement Against the Vietnam War.* New York: Monad, 1978.

Hamilton, Wallace. *Clash by Night.* Wallingford, Pennsylvania: Pendle Hill Press, 1945.

Harris, David. *Dreams Die Hard.* New York: St. Martin Press, 1983.

———. *Goliath.* New York: R. W. Baron, 1970.

Heath, G. Lewis, ed. *Mutiny Does Not Happen Lightly: The Literature of the American Resistance to the Vietnam War.* Metuchen, New Jersey: Scarecrow, 1976.

Hentoff, Nat, ed. *A. J. Muste: Essays.* Indianapolis, Indiana: Bobbs-Merrill, 1967.

Johnston, Jerome, and Bachman, Jerald C. *Young Men Look at Military Service: A Preliminary Report.* Ann Arbor, Michigan: Books on Demand, University Microfilm International, 1970.

Jones, T. Canby. *The Biblical Basis of Conscientious Objection.* Philadelphia: American Friends Service Committee, 1970.

Karnow, Stanley. *Vietnam: A History.* New York: Viking Press, 1983.

Kasinsky, Renee G. *Refugees from Militarism: Draft-Age Americans in Canada.* New Brunswick, New Jersey: Transaction Books, 1976.

Kellogg, Walter G. *Conscientious Objector.* New York: Da Capo Press, 1970.

Killmer, Richard; Lecky, Robert S.; and Wiley, Debrah C. *They Can't Go Home Again: The Story of America's Political Refugees.* Philadelphia, Pennsylvania: United Church Press, 1971.

Kohn, Stephen M. *Jailed for Peace: The History of American Draft Law Violators, 1658–1985.* Westport, Connecticut: Greenwood Press, 1986.

Kupferberg, Tuli, and Bashlow, Robert. *1001 Ways to Beat the Draft.* New York: Grove Press, 1967.

Linn, Ruth. *Not Shooting and Not Crying: Psychological Inquiry into Moral Disobedience.* Westport, Connecticut: Greenwood Press, 1989.

Little, Roger W., ed. *Selective Service and American Society.* New York: Russell Sage, 1969.

Lokos, Lionel. *House Divided: The Life and Legacy of Martin Luther King.* New Rochelle, New York: Arlington House, 1968.

Lynd, Alice, ed. *We Won't Go: Personal Accounts of War Objectors.* Boston: Beacon Press, 1968.

Lynd, Staughton, and Ferber, Michael. *The Resistance.* Boston: Beacon Press, 1971.

MacPherson, Myra. *Long Time Passing: Vietnam and the Haunted Generation.* New York: Doubleday, 1984.

Mantell, David M. *True Americanism: Green Berets and War Resisters, a Study of Commitment.* New York: Teacher's College Press, 1974.

McKeown, Bonni. *Peaceful Patriot: The Story of Tom Bennett.* Charleston, West Virginia: Mountain State Press, 1980.

Merklin, Lewis. *Those Chose Honor: The Problem of Conscience in Custody.* New York: Harper and Row, 1974.

Mitchell, Hobart. *We Would Not Kill.* Richmond, Indiana: Friends United, 1983.

Mitford, Jessica. *The Trial of Dr. Spock, The Reverend William Sloane Coffin, Jr., Michael Ferber, Mitchell Goodman, and Marcus Raskin.* New York: Knopf, 1969.

Murdock, Eugene. *Patriotism Limited, 1862–1865: The Civil War and the Bounty System.* Ann Arbor, Michigan: Books on Demand, University Microfilm International, 1967.

Murdock, Eugene C. *One Million Men: The Civil War Draft in the North.* Westport, Connecticut: Greenwood Press, 1971.

Muste, A. J. *War is the Enemy.* Wallington, Pennsylvania: Pendle Hill, 1942.

Niebanck, Richard J. *Conscience, War and the Selective Objector.* Washington, D.C.: National Interreligious Service Board for Conscientious Objectors, 1968.

Noone, Michael F., Jr., ed. *Selective Conscientious Objection: Accommodating Conscience and Security.* Boulder, Colorado: Westview Press, 1988.

Norman, E. Herbert. *Soldier and Peasant in Japan: The Origins of Conscription.* New York: AMS Press, 1943.

Olson, James S., ed. *Dictionary of the Vietnam War.* New York: Greenwood Press, 1988.

# SELECTED BIBLIOGRAPHY

O'Sullivan, John, et. al., eds. *The Draft and Its Enemies: A Documentary History*. Ann Arbor, Michigan: Books on Demand, University Microfilm International, 1974.

Peterson, Richard E., and Bilorusky, John. *The Campus Aftermath of Cambodia and Kent State*. Berkeley, California: Carnegie Commission on Higher Education, 1974.

Sale, Kirkpatrick. *SDS*. New York: Vintage, 1974.

Seeley, Robert A. *Handbook for Conscientious Objectors*. 13th ed. Philadelphia, Pennsylvania: Central Committee for Conscientious Objectors, 1981.

Seeley, Robert A., ed. *Advice for Conscientious Objectors in the Armed Forces*. 5th ed. Philadelphia, Pennsylvania: Central Committee for Conscientious Objectors, 1984.

Small, Melvin. *Johnson, Nixon, and the Doves*. New Brunswick, New Jersey: Rutgers University Press, 1988.

Spock, Dr. Benjamin. *Spock on Spock: A Memoir of Growing Up with the Century*. New York: Pantheon, 1989.

Summers, Jr., Harry G. *Vietnam Almanac*. New York: Facts on File Publications, 1985.

Surrey, David S. *Choice of Conscience: Vietnam Era Military and Draft Resisters in Canada*. New York: Praeger, 1982.

Tatum, Arlo, ed. *Handbook for Conscientious Objectors*. 10th ed., October 1968, Central Committee for Conscientious Philadelphia, Pennsylvania: Larchwood Press, Inc., 1968.

Tatum, Arlo, and Tuchinsky, Joseph S. *Guide to the Draft*. Boston: Beacon Press, 1969.

Tax, Sol, ed. *The Draft, a Handbook of Facts and Alternatives*. Chicago: University of Chicago Press, 1968.

Thoreau, Henry David. *Walden, and "On the Duty of Civil Disobedience."* New York: New American Library, 1960.

*Trials of the Resistance: Essays by Noam Chomsky, et. al.* Introduction by Murry Kempton. New York: New York Review Books, 1970.

United States Selective Service System. *Annual Reports*. Washington, D.C.: Government Printing Office, 1949–1976.

Useem, Michael. *Conscription, Protest, and Social Conflict: The Life and Death of a Draft Resistance Movement*. New York: Wiley, 1973.

———. *Protest Movements in America*. Indianapolis, Indiana: Bobbs-Merrill, 1975.

Viorst, Milton. *Fire In The Streets: America in the 1960's*. New York: Simon and Shuster, 1979.

Wall, Byron, ed. *Manual For Draft-Age Immigrants To Canada*. 5th ed. Toronto: House of Anansi, 1970.

I REFUSE

Welch, Holmes. *Taoism: The Parting of the Way.* Boston: Beacon Press, 1957.

Williams, Roger N. *New Exiles: American War Resisters in Canada.* New York: Liveright, 1971.

Wittner, Lawrence S. *Rebels Against War: the American Peace Movement, 1933–1983.* Philadelphia, Pennsylvania: Temple University Press, 1984.

*Words of Conscience: Religious Statements on Conscientious Objection.* Washington, D.C.: National Interreligious Service Board for Conscientious Objectors, 1983.

Zahn, Gordon C. *Another Part of the War: The Camp Simon Story.* Amherst, Massachusetts: University of Massachusetts Press, 1979.

Zaroulis, Nancy, and Sullivan, Gerald. *Who Spoke Up? American Protest Against the War in Vietnam 1963–1975.* New York: H. Holt and Co., 1985.

Zimmer, Timothy W. L. *Letters of a C.O. from Prison.* Valley Forge, Pennsylvania: Judson Press, 1969.

## SELECTED CASES

*Baldwin v. N.Y.,* 399 U.S. 66 (1970)

*Clay v. U.S.,* 403 U.S. 698 (1971)

*DuVernay v. U.S.,* 394 F.2d 979 (1968)

*Everett v. U.S.,* 336 F.2d 979 (1964)

*Gillette v. U.S.,* 401 U.S. 437 (1971)

*Holmes v. U.S.,* 391 U.S. 936 (1968)

*Joseph v. U.S.,* 405 U.S. 1006 (1972)

*Lowe v. U.S.,* 389 F.2d 51 (1968)

*Lutfig v. McNamara,* 373 F.2d 664 (1967)

*Mitchell v. U.S.,* 386 U.S. 972 (1967)

*Mulloy v. U.S.,* 398 U.S. 410,416 (1970)

*Petrie v. U.S.,* 407 F.2d 267 (1969)

*Sellars v. Laird,* 395 U.S. 950 (1969)

*Singer v. California,* 380 U.S. 24 (1965)

*U.S. v. Baranski,* 484 F.2d 556 (1973)

*U.S. v. Demangone,* 456 F.2d 807 (1974)

*U.S. v. Dougherty,* 473 F.2d 1113 (1972)

*U.S. v. Feliciano-Grafals,* 309 F.Supp. 1292 (1970)

*U.S. v. Freeman,* 388 F.2d 246 (1967)

*U.S. v. Garrity,* 433 F.2d 649 (1970)

*U.S. v. Heywood,* 469 F.2d 602 (1972)

*U.S. v. Houseman,* 338 F.Supp. 854 (1972)

# SELECTED BIBLIOGRAPHY

*U.S. v. Kelly*, 473 F.2d 109 (1971)
*U.S. v. Lewis*, 275 F.Supp. 1013 (1967)
*U.S. v. Mitchell*, 246 F.Supp. 874 (1965)
*U.S. v. Nelson*, 476 F.2d 254 (1973)
*U.S. v. Neptune*, 337 F.Supp. 1028 (1972)
*U.S. v. O'Brien*, 391 U.S. 367 (1968)
*U.S. v. Rauch*, 491 F.2d 552 (1974)
*U.S. v. Rehfield*, 416 F.2d 273 (1969)
*U.S. v. Rosebear*, 500 F.2d 1102 (1974)
*U.S. v. Smith*, 249 F.Supp. 515 (1966)
*U.S. v. Spock*, 416 F.2d 165 (1969)
*U.S. v. Turchick*, 451 F.2d 333 (1971)
*U.S. v. Valentine*, 288 F.Supp. 957 (1968)
*U.S. v. Vargas*, 370 F.Supp. 908 (1974)
*Williams v. Florida*, 90 S.Ct. 1893 (1970)
*Williams v. U.S.*, 406 F.2d 704 (1969)

# National Peace Organizations:
## Draft and Military Issues

American Friends Service Committee
1501 Cherry Street
Philadelphia, PA 19102
(215) 241-7000

CCCO: an Agency for Military
and Draft Counseling
2208 South Street
Philadelphia, PA 19146
(215) 545-4626

CCCO-Western Region
PO Box 42249
San Francisco, CA 94142
(415) 552-6433

Fellowship of Reconciliation
Box 271
Nyack, NY 10960-0271
(914) 358-4601

Nat'l Interreligious Service
Board for Conscientious Objectors
1601 Connecticut Ave, NW #750
Washington, DC 20009-1035
(202) 483-4510

Committee Against Registration
and the Draft
731 State Street
Madison, WI 53703
(608) 257-7562

Episcopal Peace Fellowship
620 G Street SE
Washington, DC 20003
(202) 543-7168

Women's International
League for Peace & Freedom
1213 Race Street
Philadelphia, PA 19107
(215) 563-7110

War Resisters League
339 Lafayette Street
New York, NY 10012
(212) 228-0450

Catholic Peace Fellowship
339 Lafayette Street
New York, NY 10012
(212) 673-8990

National Campaign for a
Peace Tax Fund
2121 Decatur Place, NW
Washington, DC 20008
(202) 483-3751

Midwest Committee on
Military Counseling
343 So Dearborn, Rm 1113
Chicago, IL 60604
(312) 327-5756

## VETERANS ORGANIZATIONS

Citizen Soldier
175 Fifth Avenue, Suite 808
New York, NY 10010
(212) 777-3470

Nat'l Association of Black Veterans
4185 North Green Bay Avenue
Milwaukee, WI 53209
(414) 562-VETS

Veterans for Peace
PO Box 3881
Portland, ME 04104
(207) 797-2770

Minerva Center (Women GIs)
1101 S. Arlington Ridge Rd
Arlington, VA 22202
(703) 892-4388

183

# ABOUT THE AUTHOR

Donald Laird Simons was born September 29, 1945 in Morgantown, West Virginia. He graduated from West Virginia University in 1967 with a BA in Psychology and in May 1970 with a Master of Arts in Drama. In 1981, Mr. Simons earned a Doctorate in Communication-Drama from the University of Southern California. Currently, Mr. Simons lives in Whittier, California where he is a novelist. This is his first book.

---

## FROM THE BROKEN RIFLE PRESS

The Broken Rifle Press publishe' on issues of peace, war resistance, and nonviolence. Broken Rifle strives to produce books of general interest that can also be used as supplementary reading in high school or college settings. Our guiding principle is knowledge in the interest of action and change.

**Days of Decision: an oral history of conscientious objectors in the military during the Vietnam war**
by Gerald R. Gioglio.

The peace and war stories of 24 antiwar GIs. *Days of Decision* presents a unique sociological and historical view of the Vietnam war as told by dissident soldiers. A legacy of resistance to war that celebrates the human spirit, the power of dissent and the primacy of conscience.

ISBN 0-9620024-0-2, Softcover. $14.95.

**I Refuse: memories of a Vietnam war objector**
by Donald L. Simons.

ISBN 0-9620024-2-9, Hardcover. $27.50.
ISBN 0-9620024-3-7, Softcover. $13.95.

Add $2.00 shipping, 1st book. .75 each additional.

Send to: THE BROKEN RIFLE PRESS, PO BOX 749, Trenton, NJ 08607.